THE MEANING OF THE BOULDER-DUSHANBE

Teahouse

The inspiring story of an architectural gem, a gift from Dushanbe, Tajikistan, to its American sister city, Boulder, Colorado

WRITTEN BY

George Peknik

D1405082

HOOPOE PUBLICATIONS

©2004 by Hoopoe Publications,
P.O. Box 20871, Boulder, Colorado USA 80308

Manufactured in China

ISBN 0-9632591-1-3

Book design by Rebecca Finkel, F + P Graphic Design, Inc.,
Fort Collins, Colorado; design@fpgd.com
Front cover photo courtesy of the Boulder Convention and Visitors Bureau

Distributed by
Hoopoe Publications
P.O. Box 20871
Boulder, Colorado 80308
303 883 0125 • Email geo@rmi.net

Another book by George Peknik
The Cheyenne Cañon Guidebook and Almanac

To the memory of

Mirpulat Mirakhmatov (1939–2002)

Whenever we look up, there we will see you.

Table of Contents

"A perfect falcon...

has landed on your shoulder,

and become yours."

—JELALUDDIN RUMI
The Seed Market

Introduction

In 1993, one of my English students at United Arab Emirates University wrote an account of a mosque that she said had been lifted off its foundation in her hometown of Bahla, Oman, and deposited *in toto* into a nearby city.

"You see, Allah wanted to send a message to the people of that city, Nizwa, because the people there, well, they weren't good Muslims," she explained.

During a car trip to Oman later that year, my wife Sabina and I decided to visit the two cities mentioned in the story to investigate this alleged supernatural event. First, in the *souk* area of Bahla, the "giving" city, we visited a vacant lot from which the mosque had supposedly begun its magical flight. Passers-by told us little more than *Yes, there used to be a mosque there.* That's all they knew.

The next day we visited Nizwa, the "receiving" city. A bit sheepishly, I recounted my student's tale to the desk clerk at our hotel. He said, "That would be the '*masjid-e-farfari*,' or so-called "fluttering mosque." He directed us to its location in the city center. There we found the old, small, and firmly planted domed prayer hall. I asked a nearby shop-keeper about the old mosque. He simply said that it had been a gift. That's all he knew.

My student's story is one that I clearly wouldn't expect to be duplicated anywhere else, especially in America. But three years later, shortly after moving to Boulder, Colorado, I learned about the magical journey of another building—not an Omani mosque, but a Central Asian teahouse—from a city in Tajikistan, to Boulder, Colorado, more than 7,000 miles away.

Like my student who wrote about Bahla's "fluttering mosque," I decided to research and chronicle the story of Boulder's "fluttering teahouse":
- How it "landed" in the middle of Boulder
- Where it came from
- How it has affected the more than 100,000 "pilgrims" who visit it each year
- How Boulder is reciprocating for the Teahouse with a "fluttering Cyber Cafe"

Now, I can't help but believe my Omani student's story was true. Everything has a reason. If the people in Nizwa received the mosque because they were lacking in spiritual values, what then is the message or the meaning of the gift of the Boulder-Dushanbe Teahouse?

In many countries in Asia and the Middle East, the teahouse or coffeehouse is where people go to satisfy their desire for community, peace, and enjoyment. The teahouse, or *choihona*, as it is called in Tajikistan, symbolizes very much about Tajik culture and values. It could be said that teahouses are to Central Asians what the Internet is to many Americans: a popular place to congregate and communicate, enjoy oneself, and learn about what's going on in the world and community. So, it seems rather appropriate that Boulder is reciprocating for the Teahouse with a Cyber café.

Nowadays, just about everyone in Boulder, even those who once opposed its construction, feels that it was an extraordinary gesture of international good will and generosity for the then Dushanbe Mayor Maksud Ikramov to present the Teahouse to the people of Boulder in 1987. This extraordinary gift reminds us that, as Mayor Ikramov said at the time, "When you are with friends in a teahouse, fatigue disappears."

My Reasons for Writing this Book

I have written *The Meaning of the Boulder-Dushanbe Teahouse* for four reasons:

- To inform the reader about the Teahouse's art, architecture, and gardens, and to use the building as a point of departure for exploring Persian/Tajik aesthetics, history, and culture. Perhaps by contemplating this piece of orientalia in out midst, we may better comprehend and appreciate Muslim cultures, which, for most Westerners, are a maelstrom of religious and political intrigue, distrust, confusion, and misunderstanding.

- To explore the *message* of the gift. Like the Taj Mahal, which Shah Jahan built as a love letter to his wife Momtaz, the Teahouse is a message-carrying building. Probing beneath its art and architecture reveals messages that touch on the meaning of community, friendship, pleasure, and time.

- To provide information about and to honor the many "citizen diplomats" in Boulder and Dushanbe who worked so tirelessly to facilitate a unique exchange of buildings.

- To provide information about the efforts of Boulder-Dushanbe Sister Cities to reciprocate for the gift of the Teahouse and to provide people in our Central Asian Sister City with much-needed resources and to connect the people in the two Sister Cities.

Acknowledgements

I thank the following people for their generous contributions to this project:

- My editor and dear friend, Jacqueline Frischknecht, whose wise advice, patience, guidance, and encouragement built the strength I needed to complete the project;

- My dear wife of 36 years, my best friend, and long-time fellow-traveler to the lands of the Persians and Arabs, Sabina Peknik, for the 1001 shared experiences that led to my interest in writing this book and for her valuable comments;

- My dear friend Mary Axe, whose passion for Persian and Tajik culture fuels my own, for her input on the history of the Teahouse project and its glorious art and architecture; for allowing me to use her historical photographs; and her much appreciated encouragement and advice throughout the project;
- Rebecca Finkel, for her outstanding artistic and design talents she drew on to design this book;
- Rodger Ewy, for allowing me to use his spectacular photos of the Teahouse art and architecture;
- Larry Nygaard, for his beautiful photographs of the roses;
- Professor Iraj Bashiri, for his valuable comments and suggestions on the chapter on Tajikistan and for use of his photos;
- Mikl Brawner and Jim Knopf, for their knowledgeable input on the Teahouse gardens;
- My Tajik friends Dilorom Asimova, Kholik Mirahmatov, Haydar Mirahmatov, Mirzobobo Mirahmatov, and Firuz Khalimdjonov for their information about Tajikistan, Tajiks, and Tajik teahouses;
- Mary Hey and Sophia Stoller, for their valuable comments concerning the history of the Soviet Sister City Project;
- David Barrett, for use of his schematic drawings of his remarkable design of the Cyber Café for Dushanbe;
- Barbara Perin, for her valuable comments on details of the Reciprocal Gift initiative; and
- Roger Kovacs, Emily Gianfortoni, Vern Seieroe, Lenny Martinelli, Sara Martinelli, Scott Raderstorf, Mary Hey, Gabrielle Luthy, Hartmut Bielefeldt, Nazir Sharipov, Ambassador Khamrokhon Zaripov, *The Daily Camera*, Celestial Seasonings, and The Boulder Convention and Visitors Bureau for the use of their photographs.

GEORGE PEKNIK
Boulder

PART 1

The Boulder-
Dushanbe
Teahouse

CHAPTER 1

The Art and Architecture of the Teahouse

"Great architecture is the expression of national character, the records of its experience, the declaration of its ideals... Great architecture can, like literature, be a source of infinite delight, can provide instruction, and inspiration, and favor every nation's virtue."

—ARTHUR UPHAM POPE[1]

One of the master Tajik wood carvers who created the Teahouse ceilings, Manon Khaidarov, works in his workshop in Khujand, Tajikistan.
Photo courtesy of Vern Seieroe

Dushanbe's gift to Boulder, the Boulder-Dushanbe Teahouse, or *Choihona* as it is called in the Tajiki language, is an exquisite man-made indoor garden created by master Tajik artists. Colorful painted vines meander along its hand-carved ceiling beams. Hundreds of painted flowers bathe in sunlight in a grove of carved cedar pillars. Painted birds perch in the foliage of the carved plaster and ceramic wall panels. And bronzed women draw water at a gurgling pool. Its uplifting art and architecture makes the *Choihona* a relaxing and peaceful place to drink tea, eat a meal, relax, think, and converse.

Gardens are the central theme of most Persian/Tajik artistic designs. Their representations are found in the designs of hand-knotted carpets and other textiles, metalwork, book bindings, jewelry and miniature paintings. In addition, the garden theme is prominent in the turquoise blue ceramic faience mosaics that line the walls of mosques and other buildings in Central Asia and the Middle East. It's not surprising that Tajiks and Persians fixate on gardens in their art and architecture. First, both countries have

9

desert climates, so flowers, trees, and animals are highly valued and appreciated. And second, the garden is a metaphor for the paradise where Muslims believe they will dwell in the afterlife.

What We Learn from Ornamental Details

"...An important role of ornament was to provide guidance on how people should live their lives in harmony with the world of nature and the rhythms of the universe. That we should expect such lessons from buildings seems incredible; yet before written language became a common tool for communication, buildings conveyed these messages through images carved on their walls in wood and stone."

—*Sally B. Woodbridge*[3]

On entering the Boulder-Dushanbe Teahouse, you immediately feel that you are in an extraordinary place. Your eyes are drawn upward to the elaborately carved and painted ceiling, and you are engulfed by the Teahouse's ambiance, which is created by its proportions and colors, the light, and the *gestalt* of the interior decoration, all the result of superior artistic achievement.

This serene ambiance is the result of centuries of artistic tradition. Central Asian artists have used the same elaborate architectural decoration, ornamental carving, and painting seen in the Boulder-Dushanbe Teahouse in the adornment of walls, ceilings, doors, and columns of homes, government buildings, clubs, museums, and even bus stations. This craftsmanship is executed "with an exceptional sense of tact and proportion, suggesting that one of the most amazing qualities of folk art is perhaps the ability of a décor rooted in the depths of past centuries to fit perfectly alongside the architecture of today."[2]

Lado Shanidze, the architect of the Boulder-Dushanbe Teahouse, was a Georgian who lived and worked in Dushanbe. He died in 1997, one year before it was erected.

Photo courtesy of Mary Axe

Photo courtesy of Gabrielle Luthy

Milan Milashevich's magnificent bronze sculpture "The Seven Beauties" is a focal point of the Boulder-Dushanbe Teahouse interior. It links the Choihona *to medieval Persian poetry and the rich Persian-Tajik cultural heritage.*

The Bronze Statues: "The Seven Beauties"

One of the first art objects that a visitor sees on entering the Teahouse is Milan Milashevich's "Seven Beauties" sculpture. The bronze women's graceful lines and monochrome skin, clothes, and water vessels are the perfect counterpoint for the colorful ceiling, wall decoration and furniture in the Teahouse.

"The Seven Beauties" are based on characters in the Persian romance, *Haft Paykar*, the masterpiece of Nizami Ganjavi, a native of Azerbaijan who wrote in Persian, which

The Seven Beauties Tales

The following are summaries of the seven tales spun by the princesses represented in the Teahouse pool sculptures and in the mediaeval Persian romance, *Haft Paykar*, the masterpiece of Nizami Ganjavi:

The Indian Beauty An Indian king hears of a town in China where everyone wears black. He visits it and meets the beautiful queen who withholds her love from him. The King returns to his land and then forevermore wears only black as a symbol of his sadness due to unrequited love.

The Greek Beauty A king, whose horoscope predicts danger in marriage, discards his concubines after one night. But the devoted service of one causes him to fall in love with her. She rejects him until he convinces her of his honesty and truthfulness. They marry.

The Turkish Beauty A man falls in love with a woman whose veil is briefly lifted by the wind. Unbeknownst to him, she is the wife of an acquaintance, who soon dies. Impressed by his virtue when he brings her husband's belongings to her, she agrees to marry him.

The Russian Beauty A beautiful and graceful artist feels no man is worthy of her. She shuts herself up in a fortress and declares that only he who finds a way to her will win her. A prince, after discovering the way, answers a set of riddles and wins her love.

The Moroccan Beauty Several people promise to guide an Egyptian boy, who is lost in a demon-filled desert, to safety, but don't actually do it. Finally, he appeals to God, who does guide him to safety. The boy then wears only turquoise robes of mourning in renunciation of the world.

The Chinese Beauty Good, traveling in the desert, is robbed and blinded by his companion, Bad. The daughter of a Kurdish chieftain finds and cures him. They marry and Good then becomes king and pardons Bad, who is killed by a less-forgiving King of the Kurds.

The Central Asian Beauty A young man hears music in a garden. He finds a group of maidens feasting and falls in love with one of them. His passion is returned, but their attempt at an affair is thwarted, so he decides to ask her to marry him. All ends well.

No one has been able to determine which of the seven beauties is which. This is one of the many mysteries of the Teahouse!

is closely related to Tajiki. Iranians and Tajiks regard Ganjavi as one of their own. Completed in 1197, "The Seven Beauties" recounts the history of pre-Islamic Iranian ruler Bahram Gur, who discovers a mysterious room in his palace in which there are portraits of seven princesses. Each princess is from one of the seven parts of the then-known world: India, Greece, Morocco, Persia, Khwarazm (Central Asia), Russia, China, and Rum (Byzantium, now Turkey). The pleasure-loving Bahram sends his messengers to each region to secure the princesses as his brides. His architect, Shida, builds a palace with a separate chamber for each of them. And like Scheherezade, the story-telling beauty of *The Thousand and One Arabian Nights*, each princess tells Bahram either a love story (about the frustration of unrequited love, and, less often, fulfillment), or a story of morality, virtue, or justice.

The Pool (Hauz)

The little pool in the center of the Teahouse from which the "Seven Beauties" draw water is called a *hauz* in Tajikistan. It is a traditional component of a Tajik courtyard where its water is used for a multitude of domestic purposes. Tajikistan is a dry country, so Tajiks enjoy the sound and sight of fountains, pools, and rivers. A well-known proverb in the Middle East and Central Asia is "Water is life."

Chehel Sutun *is a 17th Century garden pavilion in Isfahan, Iran, and one of that country's greatest cultural monuments. Like the Teahouse, it is surrounded by gardens, has carved wooden pillars, and was partially opened to the elements. The original architectural plans produced by Architect Lado Shanidze called for the Teahouse to have an open roof and no windows. However, the Teahouse was enclosed on site under the supervision of Vern Seieroe in order to protect it from the harsh Boulder winters. Chehel Sutun's huge* hauz, *or pool, is in front of the building, unlike the Teahouse's indoor* hauz.

Photo courtesy of Emily Wells Gianfortoni

A Grove of Pillars

A grove of twelve hand-carved, honey-colored, tapered cedarwood pillars support the Teahouse's roof. Each has a unique vegetal design with floral, vine, and leaf motifs that mirror those in the painted ceiling and carved plaster panels. This type of wooden pillar has been a mainstay of Persian-Tajik architecture for at least 2500 years. Similar wooden pillars held up some of the ceilings of the magnificent royal and sacred Achaemenid palace complex of Persepolis in what is now southern Iran. It was there that Darius the Great and Cyrus the Great held court.

One 10th century pillar from the village of Aburdon in present-day Uzbekistan can be seen in the Aibek Museum in Tashkent, Uzbekistan.[4] It resembles the pillars in the Boulder-Dushanbe Teahouse and has retained its strength, beauty and integrity as a roof support over the past millennium. The Persian Safavid shahs of the 16th century adorned the interiors of many of their palaces, mosques, and other buildings with carved wooden pillars, such as "Chehel Sutun," which means "40 Pillars," in Isfahan. That building has only 20 columns, but it stands in front of a reflecting pool which creates an illusion.

The cores of the Teahouse columns are made of steel. The cedarwood that envelopes the steel was shaped and embossed by hand. The base of each column has its own vegetal or geometrical design elements, and the pillars rise up to traditional Central Asian capitals. According to Kodir Rakhimov[6], one of the four Tajik artists who came to Boulder in 1998 to participate in the construction of the *Choihona* and to complete some of its art, the wood for the columns and for at least part of the ceiling came from the Lake Baikal region in southeast Siberia. ☛

"Because cedar is a very hard wood, at the time the Teahouse was being constructed, Tajikistan had to obtain special permission from the [Russian] military to use cedar," Kodir said. "Tajik people went to Lake Baikal area and actually selected the trees, which were then felled…It was 1988, maybe February or March."[7]

It's in the Blood

"A fondness for ornamentation seems to be an inborn characteristic of the peoples of Central Asia."[5]

The Ceiling

The ceiling of the Teahouse is the work of master Tajik woodcarvers and joiners Manon Khaidarov and the late Mirpulat Mirakhmatov, five of their fellow master wood-carvers, and six master painters.[8] The ceiling is a series of joined coffers, recessed panels. The *Choihona* has fourteen spectacular coffers, each with its own unique design of painted carved wood set between the similarly decorative ceiling beams.

Together, the coffers and ceiling beams contribute much to the ambiance of the Teahouse. They share certain design parameters with the design of Oriental carpets, and their dominant turquoise color is stunning. However, in terms of composition, motifs, color,

Photo courtesy of Rodger Ewy

and rhythm, they go their own way. In the horizontal components the designs often rely on geometric composition, as opposed to vegetal. "…Interiors shows how (Persian) artists try to express their feelings and emotions, as well as their beliefs and philosophy, through complex geometrical designs involving repetition, rhythm, pacing, scale, and color combination."[9] Along the beams, the designs are more of a vegetal, arabesque type.

Although the coffer designs vary, they are almost 100% vegetal. Turquoise, a traditional favorite color of Persian ceramicists, especially in faience mosaics of mosques and other buildings, dominates the color palette. In fact, partly because it is the color of water and is named after the word for water (obi)*, it is a favorite color throughout the Middle East and Central Asia.*

Painted hand-carved ceiling coffers have been installed in Central Asian mosques, houses, palaces, and other buildings for a millennium. In fact, the tradition of painted wood in Islamic art may have originated in Central Asia. In addition to architectural paneling, Tajik woodcarvers and painters also create beautiful furniture, musical instruments, chests, boxes, saddles, and *shebeke* (a decorative mosaic made of hundreds of inlaid patterned pieces of carved wood).[10] More recently, Tajik artisans have used them for museums, government offices, clubs, teahouses, and even metro stations.

> ### Partnering with Wood
> "When I used to come home from school, my father was always working on wood. Even my wife and children can carve. It's in our blood! When we start carving teahouses, the texture of the wood and the grain, and other characteristics of the wood—we all work together!"
>
> —*Mirpulat Mirakhmadov*[12]

"Painting on wood, as well as wood-carvings, was used for centuries not only for interior decoration, but also for the adornment of various household items. An intricate floral and geometric pattern was traced on the grounded surface of tables, caskets, boxes, saddles, and other objects. Subsequently, the pattern was painted with a thin brush; for the most part, red, green, and blue vegetable or mineral pigments were used, to which bronze and silver were added."[11]

The Ceiling Coffer Designs

Three main coffer design types are found in the Boulder-Dushanbe Teahouse:

1. The medallion design is either a recessed octagon or a square flanked by long rectangular side recessed areas, with smaller square corner recesses. An example is the coffer in the southwest corner (street side, to the far right of the entrance).
2. The polygonal design consists of parallel long rectangular or hexagonal lozenges. An example is either coffer adjacent to the coffer in the southwest corner.
3. The quasi-dome design has more deeply recessed central areas and more elaborate decoration around the coffer. The two coffers with this design are found in the places of honor, above the two entrances.

While the long beams around the large skylight do not technically comprise a coffer, they contain many of the same motifs found in the fourteen coffers.

Imaginary Flowers

Mirzobobo Mirahmatov, the grand-nephew of one of the Teahouse master woodcarvers Mirpaulat Mirahmatov, e-mailed me this note:

"The artists use their own fantasy (imagination); that is, they make the flowers larger or smaller than the same variety found in nature. Or they make them long, narrow, or wide so that the ceilings are beautiful and attractive. Such flowers as tulips, violets, and roses are frequently drawn in ceilings. Also, a variety of types of chains (zanjira) are used. For example double—twin chains (kushzanjira, literally, *"happy chains"), barley chains (javzangira), small leaf (bargak), and twin leaf (kushbargak) chains are often used."*

In the painted ceilings, the Tajik woodcarvers and painters utilized several centuries-old traditional Islamic motifs used in the designs of Oriental carpets, book bindings, ceramic tiles, and metalwork. Along the vertical walls of the ceiling coffers in the Teahouse, as shown above, are four of these motifs: From the top: stylized roses; a prayer arch, called a mihrab, *set in rows, called a* saph *in Oriental carpet design; the "tree-of-life" design and a "meander", as in the border of the Turkmen rug, upper right.*

*Overleaf, pp. **18–21**: Four of the spectacular ceiling coffers of the Boulder-Dushanbe Teahouse. Each of the fourteen coffers has a unique design that owes much to design elements and floral motifs found in Oriental carpets.*

Photo courtesy of Rodger Ewy

Photo courtesy of Rodger Ewy

Photo courtesy of Rodger Ewy

Photo courtesy of Rodger Ewy

The Carved Plaster Panels: Ganch-kori

In early 1998, after the four Tajik artisans came to Boulder to work on the Teahouse, Master Tajik plaster carver Kodir Rakhimov executed the eight spectacular *ganch* panels for the Teahouse interior in his studio on 30th and Bluff.

The time-honored process he used is fascinating. First, he created a paper pattern of his design. Next he pierced pin holes in the paper along all the design lines to trace out the motifs. The next step was to pour wet plaster into a frame. When the plaster dried to the consistency of soft cheese, he used the paper pattern and pin holes to trace the motifs onto the plaster. Using the pin holes as a guide, he carved out the design with special knives. Finally, when the panel dried, he shaped and polished the plaster. His patterns are very complex, and, unlike the Teahouse's oil paintings that he also created, conform to strict Islamic and Persian aesthetic values.

> **Self Study Plaster-carving**
>
> "When I was going to school [in Dushanbe], I started getting interested in painting...At first my parents thought that it wasn't serious and they didn't pay any attention. But afterwards, I decided art would be the serious work of my life. I went to Leningrad, and I started getting interested in plaster carving—in ganch. But it was really difficult to learn because the skilled masters would never share secrets with you and actually all ganch work was done in Tashkent [Uzbekistan] and in Tajikistan, and if you go there they wouldn't accept you as an apprentice. So I started to search in the library in Leningrad and started to work in ganch by myself as an independent artist."
>
> — *Tajik Artist Kodir Rakhimov*[13]

Carved plaster is called *ganch-kori* (in Iran, *gatch-kari*). *Ganch-kori* is a centuries-old Persian art form used for decorating wall panels and dome interiors, and, as stucco, on the exteriors of buildings. It often is mixed with ceramics and mirror work. Other than in Iran and Central Asia, it is also found in Northern Africa and southern Spain (for example, in the Alhambra in Granada, Spain). "From earliest times, stucco (and plaster)—carved, molded, and painted—was one of the major elements of Persian architectural ornament, extensively used and highly developed."[14]

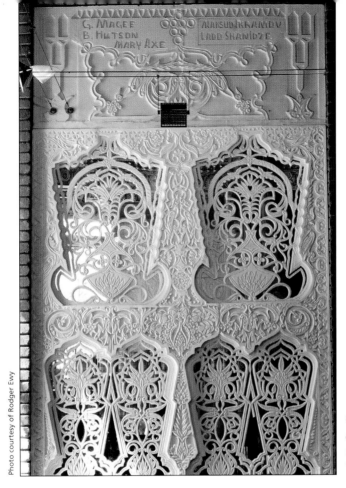

One of the spectacular carved plaster panels of the Boulder-Dushanbe Teahouse.

Looking west from the center of the Teahouse, toward the door, there are two white plaster panels. To the right (north) there is a beautiful mirrored prayer arch (*mihrab*). This design is often found in prayer carpets and represents the "gate" to heaven. It is found on the wall of mosques that Muslim worshippers face when they pray, which is oriented towards Mecca. By looking closely at the plaster panels it's possible to see half-hidden gazelles, lions, horses, and an array of floral patterns. And clearly visible is the ancient tree of life design, growing out of a vase. South of the front door the plaster panel displays a stacked *mihrab* design with peacocks. The rest of the *ganch* panels are variations on the *mihrab*, arabesque, and tree-of-life themes.

Oil Paintings

There are four abstract expressionist oil paintings executed by Kodir Rakhimov, who also did the carved plaster panels. These represent scenes of nature that encompass such diverse motifs as fish, fruit, and the sea. They are a bold juxtaposition to the rest of the *Choihona* art. It is clear from looking at his paintings that they are executed in an international style, rather than in a purely Tajik tradition. However, Kodir draws from several Tajik and Middle Eastern traditions in both his oil paintings and his carved plaster panels.

In general, his oil paintings can be grouped into four categories, including those based on Middle Eastern fables such as *1001 Arabian Nights*, those paying tribute to Omar Khayyam, The "Adam and Eve" garden of Eden series, still-lifes that incorporate traditional Tajik motifs on archeological artifacts. Just as the Teahouse has allowed us to enter into the culture of a distant and sometimes exotic culture through the mystery and power of architecture, Kodir's painting and carved plaster panels afford us a unique opportunity to explore Eastern culture through color, line, symbolism, and even literature and poetry.

Ceramic Faience Panels

Master artist Viktor Zabolotnikov and his fellow Tajik ceramicists in Dushanbe created eight wonderful faience mosaics for the four exterior walls of the *Choihona*. They were created using the same technique used to make the walls of many of the great mosques of the Middle East. Faience is a Persian invention, "which is one of the most brilliant types of architectural decoration ever used, and one of the most difficult and delicate of all ceramic arts."[15]

The technique and color scheme of the ceramic tiles used in the Boulder-Dushanbe Teahouse can be found throughout Central Asia and Iran and in the ancient architecture of the region. To make mosaic faience, the craftsman first fires tiles in different colors, then cuts them into the necessary shapes to form the desired panel. Those steps were done in Dushanbe. "The technique is difficult, extremely labor intensive, and therefore expensive, but creates faience of exceptional quality and brilliance."[16]

Each of the 6'x13' panels is organized around one of the most important designs in Islamic art, the prayer arch, or *mihrab,* framing classic Persian-Tajik vegetal and animal motifs. Because the *mihrab* is the focal point in the mosque and in the ritual of prayer one must face it during prostration, a great deal of attention has been devoted to its deco-ration in most periods throughout the Islamic world. Arabesques and other vegetal motifs are also found in the designs of the panels.

Butterflies, grapes, and grape leaves are the main design elements of the two West-facing mosaics (adjacent to the front door). The two faiences towards the front of the building on the south- and north-facing side walls exhibit

> **Pomegranates, Grapes, and Butterflies**
> "My favorite ceramic panels are the ones with the pomegranates and grapes...the butterflies came out white and I don't know why. I love the center of the panel of the pomegranates and I love the one with the grapes with the white butterflies."
> — *Tajik Master Ceramicist Viktor Zabolotnikov*[17]

eremurus (large, down-pointing strap-like flowers; also called foxtail lilies), partridges, and rosettes. Also on the south and north walls towards the back are mosaics with gladiola and butterfly designs; and in back of the building (the east side) you see the pomegranate design (with phoenix-like birds towards the north), and zinnias (or possibly double roses), 5-petal roses, and partridges.

Each of the panels has a curious ewer motif (*ibrik,* a pitcher for ritual purifications in Islam and a common motif in Islamic art) toward the top of the design. Concerning this image, ceramicist Viktor Zabolotnikov said, "It's for washing hands. It's like a symbol of ceramicists...My professor [at the art school in Dushanbe], Alnis Lipan, and I thought it would be the symbol [signature] of the ceramicists [who worked on the Boulder Teahouse project]. I even have a stamp at home [of the ewer] with my initials—ZVP...." There is an "L" for Lipan in some of the ewers on the *Choihona's* ceramic panels.[18]

Photo courtesy of Rodger Ewy

Master Tajik artist Viktor Zabolotnikov used images from nature in his eight faience panels on the outside of the Teahouse. This one features eremurus flowers framed by a prayer arch with partridges looking on.

Although the Tajik faience team fired up the panels in Dushanbe, the clay for the panels came from the Khojand area in northern Tajikistan, the same city where the *Choihona's* ceiling coffers were carved and painted. Viktor said, "When two trucks left from Dushanbe to take wood to [ceiling woodworkers] Manon and Mirpulat, I phoned Khojand to request that the trucks return with the clay…they sent me 24 tons of clay. And ever since I have been using that clay [for other projects]."[19]

The Choihona's *Persian Traditions*

Visitors to the Boulder-Dushanbe Teahouse often ask the wait staff about the type of art and architecture that makes up the Teahouse. Is it Russian? Islamic? Chinese? Persian?

The answer has everything to do with who the Tajiks are. They are a Persian people, meaning they speak a variety of Farsi (which is also called Persian). They trace their ancestry back to ancient Persia, unlike the majority of the inhabitants of neighboring countries, such as Uzbekistan and Kazakhstan, who are Turkish. As the borders of the Persian Empire (550-330 B.C.) and the subsequent Persian dynasties ebbed and flowed over much of the Middle East and Central Asia, the excellence of Tajikistan's artistic traditions and the robustness of its culture had a profound effect throughout Asia.

More than 400 miles of mountains and desert separate Tajikistan from Iran. But largely because of geography and the invention of foreign armies throughout the last millennium, the people of the two countries have not had close relations over the years. However, in addition to being heavily influenced by Russian culture, Tajikistan has been influenced by its neighbors, including the Chinese, Uzbeks, and Kazakhs. Consequently, although their art, architecture, music, language, and literature share characteristics with the Iranians and others, they have developed their own distinctive aesthetic values and national identity.

> **Paying It Forward**
> "The teahouse is like a flower. We hope it brings people happiness and enjoyment. People will come, drink coffee or tea, and look up—and it will make their souls happy."
> —*Mirpulat Mirakhmatov, master Tajik woodcarver*

Tajikistan has a rich artistic heritage that goes back at least 2000 years. Religion is an important inspiration for art everywhere, and much of the art of Tajikistan and Central Asia is religious in origin. The religious influence is evident in the extravagant gigantic Buddhist statuary, in murals and in the Zoroastrian fire temples. Wonderful examples can also be found in illustrated Islamic texts, metalwork, and the glazed tile work of mosques.

Photo courtesy of Emily Wells Gianfortoni

The Choihona *follows the tradition of 2500 years or Persian art and architecture that includes this mosque, The Imam Mosque in Isfahan, Iran. It was built in the 11th century. Tajik art makes us feel deeply and intensely through its imagery, which, like the* Choihona's *art, often includes flowers and other scenes of nature and embraces a spiritual quality.*

The Original Teahouse Plan vs. Today's Teahouse

An interesting footnote in the construction of the Boulder-Dushanbe Teahouse is that the original architectural plans, drawn up by the late architect Lado Shanidze, called for the Teahouse interior to be almost completely open to the elements. There were to be no windows, and surprisingly only a partial ceiling, extending no more than 10 feet inwards from the walls. Boulder architect Vern Seieroe added the closed ceiling and windows to make the building suitable for Colorado weather.

While many people have puzzled over the fact that the building was envisioned by the architect to be *al fresco*, there is actually a very good explanation. Because the Persians and Tajiks love the out-of-doors and gardens so much, there is a strong tradition of exposing interiors of buildings including mosques, teahouses and homes. (A comparable phenomenon is the interior *placita* courtyards or open-porch *portals* of Mexico and New Mexico.) Teahouses in Dushanbe, such as the famous *Saodat Choihona*, are in fact open on both levels. Teahouse customers are warmed by hot tea at outdoor tables.

An example of the blurring of the line between "outside" and "inside" can be found in the Ali Qapu palace in Isfahan, Iran. "It is tall, square in plan…with the *talar* (open porch with columns)as the second story…capable of holding two or more courtiers… The interior is covered with murals, all rendered in polychrome relief. Many small rooms for private entertainment have fireplaces and are open on one side, evidencing again the Persian technique of bringing the out-of-doors into their houses."[20]

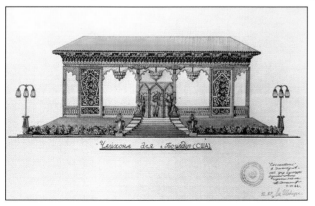

Project Architect Georgian Lado Shanidze's original plan called for an open air pavilion-like building with a tiny kitchen.

Five Special Details of the Teahouse

The Hidden Peacock

High on the center pillar along the south wall (to the right as you enter) hides a peacock that was serendipitously inserted by one of the wood-carvers. The peacock is an important symbol in Islamic art.

The Show Case

Just to the right of the entrance of the Teahouse there is a display case with a number of interesting artifacts that reflect Tajik culture. Included in this display are a brass Russian samovar (a water boiler used for heating water for tea in Central Asia, Russia, the Caucuses, and Iran); a Tajik woman's wedding gown and crown, which was donated by BDSC Board Member Sophia Stoller, who had received the two items from a Tajik government official on one of her many trips to Tajikistan; a Tajik man's ceremonial robe (called a *chapan*), which was presented to the late Dr. Stan Brenton, a general surgeon, on the occasion of his 60th birthday by his Tajik friend Izatullo Khoshmukhamedov; ceramic plates; and other miscellaneous artifacts that reflect Tajik culture. William Scott, a local craftsman, built the show case, the bar, and the tables with inlaid ceramic tiles with the Farsi words for tea and friendship-related concepts, including, "peace" *(sohl),* "tea" *(choi),* "love" *(eshq),* and "friendship" *(dusti).*

The Kats (also called Chorpois)

Another special feature of the *Choihona* is the two low tables in the corners on the north side of the room where diners may sit. These *kats* (or *chorpois*) are traditional Central Asian chairs. (The Russian word *"topchan"* is also used.) There are also a number of smaller tables with stools on the south side. All of this furniture is painted with traditional motifs that resemble some of the themes in the ceiling coffers.

The Suzani

There is a long, approximately 20-foot embroidered hanging on the east wall, near the door leading to the kitchen, called a *suzani,* or *suzaneh.* These sophisticated embroideries are used during wedding ceremonies to decorate interiors and to divide a backyard into separate spaces for different groups of guests. *Suzanis* sometimes are a part of a girl's dowry and are prepared by the bride and her relatives long before the wedding. Smaller ones may be used as regular tablecloths or doilies.

This striking *suzani* exhibits a large traditional symmetrical circle motif, called a *shams* (sun). It was a gift (shortly after the Teahouse opening) from a group of Tajik business people who had been in touch with The Rotary Club of Boulder. Norris Hermsmeyer, past President of The Rotary Club of Boulder, presented the gift to the *Choihona.*

The Inscriptions

The inscriptions, which cover much of the upper sections of the walls and beams in the *Choihona,* are another special feature. There are two basic types. One type found on the plaster panels lists some of the people who were instrumental in having the Teahouse built. They are written in English script.

There are five names on the plaster panel to the north (right) of the door as you face it from the interior:

Kodir Rakhimov, who created the carved plaster panels, as well as the oil paintings

Vern Seieroe, the Boulder architect who modified the original architectural drawings so that they would conform to local code and needs

David Robertson, who, with his wife Janet, hosted Kodir Rakhimov during part of his stay in Boulder

Lenny Martinelli, who worked as a volunteer in the construction phase and went on to become the Teahouse's proprietor

Jamshid Drakhti, an Iranian resident of Boulder County, who worked with the Boulder construction team and often translated for the Tajik artisans (two of whose names are inscribed on the coffer beams along the east wall)

There are five names on the plaster panel to the south of the door as you face it from the interior:

Maksud Ikramov, the late distinguished mayor of Dushanbe, whose idea it was to give the *Choihona* to the city

Lado Shanidze, the chief architect of the *Choihona,* a native of Georgia, the former Republic of the Soviet Union, and long-time resident of Dushanbe

G. Magee, Boulder City Project Manager from Facilities Asset Management

B. Hutson, Boulder City Project Manager from Facilities Asset Management

Mary Axe, the former President of Boulder-Dushanbe Sister Cities, who was largely responsible for getting the Teahouse built as Chair of the Teahouse Trust

continued on page 33

continued from page 32

Carved onto the sides of the first coffer (from the south wall) above the bar are the names of three master Tajik wood-carvers who worked on the Teahouse: **Gaibulo Akhmadchonov, Yusufchon Mirakhmatov,** and **Dadochon Butorov.** Carved onto the middle coffer above the back door are names of three other master Tajik wood-carvers: **Abdumannon Khaidarov, Mirpulat Mirakhmatov,** and **Valichon Temurov.**

There is an interesting painted inscription on the green plaque above the back door in Cyrillic, which is written left to right and uses characters that resemble English but is stylized to look like Arabic, which is written right to left. It says:

Master Craftsmen of Tajikistan
From the city of Leninabad (a.k.a. Khujand).
Constructed in the year 1988.

The Master Painters:
Akhrorov, Azam   Khakaisov, M.   Nurmatov, I.
Kudratov, Kh.   Aliev, K.   Azimov, A.   Pulatov, A.

The ceiling coffer in the northeast corner is inscribed on four sides with what can be translated as:

Master craftsmen of exceptional talent
from the old town of Khujand create magic.

The final inscription can be seen on a west-facing beam north of the entrance. Written in Arabic, it says, *"Allah Akbar,"* which means "God is great". *(Translations courtesy of Mary Axe)*

An inscription along a ceiling beam at the back of the Choihona *says: "Master craftsmen of Tajikistan from the city of Leninabad (a.k.a. Khujand). Constructed in the year 1988," followed by their names (see left).*

One of the Choihona's *'Seven Beauties'*

Photo courtesy of Rodger Ewy

Vern Seieroe

Boulder resident and architect Vern Seieroe, A.I.A., supervised the redesign and construction of the Boulder-Dushanbe Teahouse. He traveled with the first official delegation from Boulder to visit Tajikistan in 1988 when he discussed the assembly of the Teahouse with his Dushanbe colleague, Lado Shanidze. Vern donated many hours to the project and, as the lead architect, designed the up-to-code kitchen, restrooms, windows, ceiling, and front-door access ramp. He also chose the lighting fixtures, and electrical and plumbing fixtures. Vern is also a leader in the effort to construct Boulder's gift to Dushanbe, a Cyber Café learning center (see Chapter 7).

Here are some of Vern's comments about the Teahouse:

• *"The gift of the Teahouse was a stroke of genius. Any artistic gift from Boulder to Dushanbe would have to be in memory of former Dushanbe Mayor Ikramov and Teahouse Architect Lado Shanidze, who both died in 1997, shortly before we broke ground. The gift has bound the two cities in spirit."*

• *"Our first challenge was to take the open-air design and enclose it so that it could be used during Boulder winters. Lighting was a major design issue because we had to light the interior but not distract from the artwork. Every decision was always made in consideration of the question, 'Will this detract from the artwork?'"*[21]

• *"I have nothing but admiration for the Tajik craftsmen who worked on the Teahouse. For example, none of the ceiling pieces or the columns warped, either in transit or during seven years' storage. In a building, if the diagonals are the same, it's square and accurate. The Teahouse ceiling was square to within ¼ of an inch, so it was built to tighter tolerances than we normally use in the US."*[22]

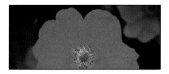

Bogh

CHAPTER 2

The Teahouse Gardens

"Can you find another market like this?
Where, with your one rose,
you can buy hundreds of rose gardens"
—JELALUDDIN RUMI, *The Seed Market*

The first experience a visitor to the Teahouse enjoys, especially in summer, is a walk through the Teahouse gardens. The closer one walks to the Teahouse entrance, the higher the roses reach. The effect is like walking down a fragrant, colorful corridor. The garden's more than fifty species of roses and numerous other plantings foreshadow the Teahouse's "inside garden" of art. The *Choihona*'s gardens were the result of efforts of the Boulder Garden Club and the Boulder Valley Rose Society. Their members donated much time, expertise, plantings, and materials before the Teahouse opened its doors in May 1998.

The rose garden is a demonstration garden for rose-lovers. It is in fact called the "Hardy Rose Demonstration Garden of the Boulder Valley Rose Society" and is an environment that delights the senses and calms the spirit, such as you might find outside a Central Asian teahouse. It includes over 49 varieties of roses of many types, including Old Garden roses, Species roses, Canadian, climbing, and David Austin's English roses. The Rose Garden was designed by Eve Reshetnik and Mikl Brawner of Harlequin's Gardens. It was intended to look "unplanned" in the Tajik tradition and to create a sensual, perfumed, and intimate atmosphere. Eve is a landscape architect and an acclaimed botanical artist who is very knowledgeable about heirloom roses. Mikl is a nurseryman who has experience growing Canadian Roses and shrub roses under difficult conditions. Together they are owners of Harlequin's Gardens, a Boulder plant nursery specializing in Colorado-adapted plants, hardy own-root roses, natives and xeriscape plants.

Mikl said his research led him to believe that among the varieties represented at the Teahouse, the following have relatives in or around Dushanbe:

- Persian Yellow, a variant of *Rosa. foetida*, it has double yellow blooms
- Austrian Copper, an orange-yellow shrub
- *Kazanlik ("The Rose of Shiraz"), a double pink rose*
- *Rose de Rescht*, a deep magenta-color, it is an Old Garden Rose known for its especially sweet fragrance

Mikl and Eve agreed it was important that all the roses be on their own roots. In general, most roses are grafted onto a vigorous rootstock, because this method produces greater numbers of roses, faster. However there are serious disadvantages. The graft is more cold-sensitive than any other part, and if the graft and top die, the rootstock rose will come up instead. By using own-root roses, the plants would be stronger, healthier and longer-lived.

Photo courtesy of Larry Nygaard

*Four species of roses found in the Boulder-Dushanbe Teahouse Rose Garden
(from upper left, clockwise): Abraham Darby, Gourmet Popcorn, Robusta, and Louise Odier.*

Roses have long been associated with Tajik and Persian culture. The great Persian poets, such as Omar Khayyam, Saadi, and Hafez, frequently alluded to the rose. Carpet-designers and other Persian artisans have often included the rose in their designs. Saadi's most famous work is entitled Gulistan ("The Rose Garden"). Vegetal motifs are also found in most examples of Islamic art. More than 95% of all oriental carpet designs, for example, portray a garden, both abstract and representational.

Preparing and Maintaining the Teahouse Rose Garden

The soil that was brought in for the garden was the usual clayey topsoil which holds water well and is rich in minerals. But because it was very heavy and did not allow enough oxygen to the roots, several yards of compost were tilled in. Then in May 1998 members of the Boulder Valley Rose Society donated and planted the roses using Mile-Hi Rose Feed and alfalfa meal.

The city of Boulder installed a micro sprayer irrigation system to keep water from being sprayed on the leaves, which can cause fungus problems. Since then the Rose Society has maintained the garden using organic methods. The results have been beyond everyone's expectations. Not only have the plants grown rapidly, but thankfully, they have been very healthy, and the colors and fragrances are deeply satisfying.

Beyond the Roses

Boulder xeriscape architect Jim Knopf was also central to the creation of the Teahouse gardens. In the late 1980's, Jim participated in a BDSC-sponsored tour to Tajikistan, and he later developed the non-rose plant list. Jim is a member of the Boulder Garden Club (BGC) and worked closely with then BDC President Mary Kirk and other BGC members, including June Holmes and Jeannette George.

> "The Gardens of the Persians commonly consist of one Great Walk, which parts the Garden... planted with fruit trees and rose bushes..."
> —Sir John Chardin,
> *Travels in Persia 1673- 1677*

Two of the plantings currently scaling the pergolas—wild grape and *clematis tanguitica* —can also be found in Tajik gardens and canyons. Other plants on their way up the pergolas are another species of clematis, porcelain vine. American wisteria, whose graceful spiraling cone-shaped flowers are reflected in the ceramic panels on the north- and south-facing exterior walls of the *Choihona*, add even more beauty.

According to Jim, author of *The Xeriscape Flower Gardener: A Waterwise Guide for the Rocky Mountain Region,* and chief designer and cultivator of the non-rose plants in the *Choihona* garden, there are several species of plants in the Teahouse garden that also grow in Tajikistan:

- *Potentilla fruiticosa,* Fireweed (*Epilobium angustifolium*), *Juniperus communis, Polygonum* balschuanica (*Buchara fleecevine*), Tunic Flower (*Petrorhagia saxafraga*), *Iris bucharaca,* and Giant Ornamental Onion (*Allium giganteum*).

- Jim planted our North American Aspen in the Teahouse garden. In Tajikistan there is an extremely close species. The Boulder variety is *Populus tremuloides,* and the Tajik "sister-aspen" is *Populus tremula.*

Photo courtesy of Larry Nygaard

- Jim also planted our native Columbine (*Aquilegia coerulea*). Tajikistan has other native Columbines.

- Similar varieties of grapes grow in Tajikistan.

The *Choihona:* In a Neighborhood of Gardens

The Boulder-Dushanbe Teahouse Garden is one of several gardens near Boulder Creek and its branches. Others include:

The Peace Garden is located between the Municipal Building and the Boulder Public Library just west of Broadway. It was planted in 1989 to display native wildflowers from Boulder and its Sister Cities. (A five minute walk from the *Choihona*.)

The Boulder Creek Xeriscape Garden is located just west of the Justice Center on Canyon and 5th Avenue. One-fourth acre, featuring 6 turf types and 75 species of plants, including herbs, interpretive signs and labeled plants. (A 15 minute walk from the *Choihona*.)

The AIDS Memorial Garden is located one-half block east of Broadway, south of Arapahoe, just about one block south of the *Choihona*. (A five minute walk from the *Choihona*.)

The Municipal Building Garden is located on the west side of Broadway, just west of the *Choihona*. (A five minute walk from the *Choihona*.)

The Andrews Arboretum is located on the east side of Broadway between Grandview and Marine, about 5–6 blocks south of the *Choihona*. It was established in 1948 by former Boulder High School botany teacher Maud Reed. It is open everyday free of charge. For more information, or to schedule a tour, contact the Forestry section of the City of Boulder Parks and Recreation Department at 303-441-4407, Monday – Friday, 7:00 am – 3:30 pm. (A 15 minute walk from the *Choihona*.)

The Environmental Defense Fund Garden is located on the northeast corner of Arapahoe and 14th, about one block from the Teahouse. It features wildflowers and grasses native to Colorado.

The Butterfly Garden is located at the creek just east of 6th Street. (Due west of the *Choihona*, it is about a 15 minute walk from the *Choihona*) Boulder County Youth Corps constructed this garden that attracts butterflies in 1997–1998.

Not too far from the creek area is the **Colorado Shakespeare Gardens** on the Colorado University campus. First planted in 1992, the Colorado Shakespeare Gardens feature plants mentioned in Shakespeare's timeless plays. The highlight garden is planted each year with a selection of herbs, flowers and vegetables mentioned in the season's plays. For information, visit www.coloradoshakes.org. (A 20–30 minute walk from the *Choihona*.)

One of the first signs of spring in Boulder is the emergence of the tulips on Pearl Street Mall, all 15,000 of them. The annual **Tulip Festival**, usually in late April, features the flowers, jazz, and a Tulip Fairy Parade. (The famous Pearl Street Mall is two blocks north of the *Choihona*.)

The Earliest Gardens

It is believed that the world's first planned gardens were created in Iran as early as the sixth Century B.C. A garden surrounded the tomb of Cyrus the Great at Pasargadae in what is now southern Iran hundreds of years before Christ. Throughout the centuries since then, gardens, roses, and other flowers have been praised by poets of the region. In the Koran paradise is a garden.

Vita Sackville West visited Persia in 1927 and contributed a chapter on Persian Gardens to Arberry's *The Legacy of Persia* in 1953. Her summary of the characteristics of Persian gardens reflect those of the Boulder-Dushanbe Teahouse:

"All Persian gardens are walled in. It is part of their character... we may safely say that the layout was always more or less the same: the long avenues, the straight walks, the summer-house or pavilion at the end of the walk, the narrow canals running like ribbons over blue tiles, widening out into pools which oddly enough were seldom circular, but more likely to be rectangular, square, octagonal, cross-shaped, or with tri-lobed or shamrock-like ends. Sometimes these pools were reproduced inside the pavilion itself: a mirror of water beneath a domed roof, fantastically reflecting all the honeycomb elaboration of the ceiling." (pp. 267-268)

Paradise as a Garden

The Koran provides a clear vision of Paradise in natural terms to its readers. The most compelling example is in Sura 76 (Verses 5-6):

"...and [God] recompensed them for their patience with a garden and silk;

therein they shall recline upon couches

therein they shall see neither sun nor bitter cold,

near them shall be its shades, and its clusters hang meekly down

and there shall be passed around them vessels of silver, and goblets of crystal,

crystal or silver that they have measured very exactly.

And therein they shall be given to drink a cup whose mixture is ginger,

Therein a fountain whose name is Salsabil."

Ice-skating at the Choihona in 2000.

The Teahouse Trail

Adding to the outdoor ambiance of the Boulder-Dushanbe *Choihona* is a branch of Boulder Creek, which rushes south of the *Choihona*. It contributes another very Tajik touch to the setting.

The bridge and the creek-side Teahouse Trail round out the outdoor features of the Teahouse. Visiting master ceramicist Victor Zabolotnikov and Boulder artist Aprylisa Snyder created the ceramic mythical Tajik birds on the bridge. Aprylisa also created the lovely Omar Khayyam quatrains from *The Rubaiyat* set into the walk in both Persian and English (see photo). To do so she first copied the text from a book then enlarged the words so they could be sandblasted into the rock.

One of Aprylisa Snyder's Teahouse Trail tiles with a verse from Omar Khayyam's Rubaiyat.

In the idealized classic setting for a Persian picnic, as expressed in Omar Khayyam's "a jug of wine (fun), a loaf of bread (food), and thou (companionship)," the other components are a tree (shade, comfort) and a stream (nature's bounty). Omar Khayyam, Persian astronomer, mathematician, philosopher, and poet, lived in Nishapur, in what is now north-eastern Iran, only a few hundred miles from present-day Tajikistan. He lived in the second half of the 11th and first quarter of the 12th century. In his many quatrains, he wrote of the joys of wine, savoring the moment, the brevity of life, and love.

According to Aprylisa, the Teahouse Trail was intended to express the unity of the two sister cities. She and Tajik artist Kodir Rakhimov collaborated on the bridge decks on the west end of the trail. They were conceived as flying carpets to symbolize the "magical" journey one takes when going from one culture to the other. The red carpets are fringed with tile on either end, embellished with bird motifs at opposing corners, and the center of each carpet bears a stylized map with the location of each city indicated by a flower. Doves rest on the corners. Tajik ceramic artist Victor Zabolotnikov, creator of the Teahouse facade tiles, created the Balustrade tiles also with bird motifs of birds.

As you face the Teahouse the center portion of the carpet bears a stylized map of Colorado with a Columbine blossom indicating Boulder. The patterns at each corner of the diamond shaped map area are direction indicators from an astrolabe, an instrument for observing or showing the positions of the stars invented by Muslim scientists more than 1200 years ago.

Aprilysa said that the east bridge represents Tajikistan. As you face the Teahouse the Central Asian country is outlined and a tulip indicates the location of Dushanbe. The motifs on each corner are mythical bird from Persian folklore, possibly the *simorgh*.

As if blown by a breeze, impressed oak leaves are scattered across the path. The oak is a symbol of fidelity and is thus a reminder of the friendship of the two sister cities.

The Teahouse poem by Omar Khayyam, quoted from *The Rubaiyat*, includes Solomon's star motifs set in diamond shapes. This star pattern is a common motif found in Persian art, ceramics and architecture. Each pattern contains elements held by Jewish, Muslim and Christian cultures. The poem is scripted in English reading west to east and in Farsi from east to west. The center diamond features a teapot.

The attention paid to the creation of the exterior surroundings of the Teahouse adds immeasurably to this wonderful gift from the people of Dushanbe. By creating a garden, placing the Teahouse by a stream, and creating outdoor dining space, Boulderites have insured that the entire Teahouse site is reflective of traditional Central Asian teahouses.

The Omar Khayyam quatrains along the Teahouse Trail sidewalk include these two:

And those who stood before
The Teahouse shouted - Open the door!
You know how little time we have to stay
And once departed, may return no more.

Here beneath the bough,
A loaf of bread, a flask of wine and thou,
Singing beside me in the wilderness
And wilderness is paradise now.

Almost every oriental carpet design represents a garden. Note the many original floral motifs in the 18 rectangles in the field and cartouches in the border of this 19th century Iranian tribal Bahktiari "Garden Compartment" carpet.

An Interview with Mikl Brawner about the Teahouse Rose Garden

Mikl Brawner and Eve Reshetnik are co-owners of Harlequin's Gardens and co-designer of the Boulder-Dushanbe Teahouse Rose Garden.

Question: Why did you want to get involved with this project?
Mikl: It was the beauty and craftsmanship of the Teahouse itself, coupled with the spirit of peace and generosity of the Tajik people, that inspired us to put so many hours into the design of the rose garden. We wanted it to be both complementary to the teahouse and highly successful as a rose demonstration garden.

Question: How did you and Eve choose the rose varieties for the Teahouse Garden?
Mikl: We chose the roses according to: cold-hardiness; fragrance; disease resistance; bloom sequence, size, and color—and the probability of their presence in Tajikistan. We worked with then-Rose Society President Dawn Penland and other members of the organization.

Question: Which varieties do Teahouse visitors most ask or comment about?
Mikl: Golden Wings is perhaps the most asked about rose. Even though it is only 50 years old it does not look modern. It is a single rose with large yellow to cream petals and show mahogany stamens. It repeat blooms very well and is sweetly scented. It also has show rose hips, and is very reliable. Rose de Rescht is said to come from Persia. It is one of the best old roses in that it is deliciously fragrant, has a compact 4' form and repeats very reliably. The 3" magenta-red flowers are very double and make a perfect boutonniere. "Victorian Memory" is a very unusual rose in that it is a very cold hardy climber that both repeats and is fragrant. The bright lilac-pink nodding flowers are profuse and the canes can reach the second story of a house. Kazanlik is a very ancient Damask rose with warm pink, double old-fashioned flowers that are very fragrant. It is used in making the famous Bulgarian Attar (essence) of Roses.

Question: What factors did you take into consideration for the garden with respect to the Teahouse itself?
Mikl: We felt that the modern hybrid tea and floribunda roses would have been out of character with the "Old World" atmosphere, and they would not have been hardy enough. We chose roses that are real shrubs that produce greater volumes of flowers that have good fragrance and old-fashioned forms. This helped to create privacy and intimacy. In addition, because the Teahouse is a public place where people dine, we made a commitment to not using any toxic pesticides.

Question: When is the best time of year to view the roses?
Mikl: The roses bloom from June through September, but my favorite time is June when the once-blooming varieties create an experience that is unforgettable. There's an environment of fragrance and splendor that goes way beyond "pretty" into passionate and...intoxicating! Quite a way to enter that beautiful teahouse!

Rose Garden Map

Abbreviations: AUS = David Austin English rose; **B** = Griffith Buck hardy rose; **CAN** = Canadian-bred hardy rose; **CL** = Climber; **f** = lightly fragrant; **F** = fragrant; **FF** = very fragrant; **HP** = hybrid perpetual; **OGR** = Old Garden Rose; **POL** = Polyantha; **R** = repeat-blooming; **SH** = shrub; **sl.** = single; **dbl.** = double

1. **Constance Spry** (SH/CL, AUS, FF, dbl. pink)
2. **William Lobb** (SH/CL, OGR, Moss, FF, dbl. mauve-purple)
3. **Rosa Setigera** (SH/CL, Species, sl. pink, blooms July)
4. **Golden Wings** (SH, Modern, F, R, sl. lt. yellow, red stamens)
5. **Mme. Hardy** (SH, OGR, Damask, FF, dbl. white)
6. **Louise Odier** (SH, OGR, Bourbon, FF, R, dbl. pink)
7. **Abraham Darby** (SH, AUS, FF, R, dbl. apricot-pink)
8. **Winchester Cathedral** (SH, AUS, f, R, dbl. white)
9. **Rose de Rescht** (SH, OGR, Portland, FF, R, deep magenta)
10. **Gros Choux de Hollande** (SH, OGR, Centifolia, FF, dbl. av-pink)
11. **Sydonie** (SH, OGR, HP, FF, R, dbl. pink)
12. **Gourmet Popcorn** (SH, POL, R, small dbl. white)
13. **Fru Dagmar Hastrup** (SH, Rugosa Hybrid, F, R, sl pink)
14. **Robusta** (SH/CL, Rugosa Hybrid, R, deep crimson)
15. **Sparrieshoop** (SH, Kordesii Hybrid, f, R, sl. lt. pink)
16. **J.P. Connell** (SH/CL, CAN, R, lt. yellow-white)
17. **Ferdinand Pichard** (SH, 0GR, HP, F, R, dbl. striped crimson-pink)
18. **Persian Yellow** (SH, OGR, Species Hybrid, dbl. bright yellow)
19. **William Baffin** (SH/CL, CAN, R, sl pink, white center)
20. **Rosa Glauca** (SH, Species, single pink, showy foliage/fruit)
21. **Kazanlik** (SD, OGR, Damask, FF, dbl. pink)
22. UNKNOWN SPECIES
23. **Austrian Copper** (SH, Species, OGR, bright orange-yellow)
24. **Victorian Memory** (SH/CL, f, R, dbl. pink)
25. **Gertrude Jekyll** (SH/CL, AUS, FF, R, deep pink)
26. **Theresa Bugnet** (SH, Rugosa Hybrid, F, R, dbl. pink)
27. **John Davis** (SH/CL, CAN, F, R, dbl. pink)
28. **Felicite Parmentier** (SH, OGR, Alba Hybrid, FF, blush-white)
29. **L.D. Braithwaite** (SH, AUS, f, R, crimson)
30. **Rose de Rescht** (see 9)
31. **Sydonie** (see 11)
32. **Scharlachglut** (SH/CL, Kordesii Hybrid, single crimson)
33. **Alba Suaveolens** (SH, OGR, Alba, F, dbl. white, fruit)
34. **Graham Thomas** (SH, AUS, F, R, dbl. yellow)
35. **Banshee** (SH, OGR, Found, FF, dbl. pink, fall color)
36. **Mme. Plantier** (SH/CL, OGR, Alba Hybrid, FF, dbl. white)
37. **Othello** (SH, AUS, FF, R, crimson)
38. **Golden Wings** (see 4)
39. **Abraham Darby** (see 7)
40. **Rose de Rescht** (see 9)
41. **Morden Blush** (SH, CAN, R, dbl. blush pink)
42. **Gourmet Popcorn** (see 12)
43. **Dart's Dash** (SH, Rugosa, FF, R, lg. sl. magenta, lg. fruit)
44. **Applejack** (SH, B, f, R, single pink)
45. **Rosa Glauca** (see 20)
46. **Persian Yellow** (see 18)
47. **Rosa Glauca** (see 20)
48. **Lillian Gibson** (SH, semi-dbl. lt. pink)
49. **Salet** (SH, OGR, Moss, F, R, dbl. pink)
50. **Winnipeg Parks** (SH, CAN, R, semi-dbl. red-pink)
51. **William Baffin** (See 19)
52. **Goldbusch** (SH/CL, Eglantaria Hybrid, f, R?, lt. gold-apricot)
53. **Crested Jewel** (SH, Moss, F, bright pink)
54. **Lawrence Johnston** (CL, Spinosissima Hybrid, FF, R, blush)
55. **Seafoam** (SH/CL, groundcover, R, small dbl. white-blush)
56. **Bonica** (SH, f, R, dbl. pink, fruit)
57. **Stanwell Perpetual** (SH, OGR, Spinosissima Hybrid, FF, R, blush)
58. **Rosa Mundi** (SH, OGR, Gallica, F, striped crimson/white)

The Boulder-Dushanbe Teahouse

Rose Garden

see page 51 for annotations and varieties

gate

Teahouse

PART 2

The Cultural Context of the Boulder-Dushanbe Teahouse

Photo courtesy of Scott Raderstorf

Choihona

CHAPTER 3

Central Asian Teahouses

"The tea-room...an oasis in the dreary waste of existence where weary travelers could meet to drink from the common spring of art appreciation."

—KAZUKO OKAKURA[23]

Teahouses and their coffeehouse cousins exist in most countries of the world, but how they look and are organized varies considerably. Their varieties include the ubiquitous Starbucks, the modest mountain-trekkers' tea-room, the urban Internet café, and the tradition-rich Japanese garden teahouse. Although they are places where people gather to drink hot caffeinated beverages, that's about all they have in common.

The Asian teahouse is a social institution that is the center of daily life for many people (usually men) from Istanbul to Tokyo. During the last hundred years, it has survived the popularity of the radio, the television, the telephone, the cinema, the Internet, tobacco, alcohol, drugs, McDonalds, Coca-cola *and* Starbucks. Teahouses are to Central Asians what the Internet has become to many Americans: a place to congregate and communicate with others, have fun, and learn about what's going on in the world and in one's town. Asians visit teahouses not only to drink tea, but also to refresh and energize themselves, to exchange news and gossip, and to seek diversion from the bustle or boredom of work, society, or home.

Origins of Teahouses

The first teahouses appeared in Japan in the 16th century. Soon after that, both teahouses and coffeehouses became popular meeting places in Central Asia, the Middle East, and later Europe. In what probably is the first report by a European of an Asian teahouse, Frenchman Sir Thomas Herbert described the social scene of an early 17th century coffeehouse in Isfahan, Iran:

> "...near the entrance to the bazaars were the coffee-houses, which at seven or eight o'clock in the morning were already full of coffee-drinkers and tobacco-smokers. The guests sat in a circle, in the middle of which stood a large vessel of water for cleaning of foul pipes. [Shah] Abbas the Great, finding that the coffee-houses were becoming hotbeds of political intrigue, directed that a mulla should be in permanent attendance to deliver to these Tobacco-whiffers and Coffee-quaffers edifying lectures on history, poetry, or the law."[24]

The samovar is used to boil water for making tea in the Middle East, Central Asia, Russia, and some other countries of the former Soviet Union. Not all Tajiks use a samovar these days. Gas stoves and electric kettles are superseding this old traditional boiler, especially in the larger cities. This man is selling tea in Dushanbe's open-air Saodat Teahouse in winter.

A teahouse in Tajikistan is called a *choihona* (literally, "teahouse"), while in Iran it is called a *gahveh-khane*, which literally means "coffeehouse," even though people normally drink tea there. Some Asian teahouses are not much more than a collection of a few tables and chairs along a sidewalk and an entrepreneur with a samovar. Others sit proudly on fashionable boulevards. Some, like the *Saodat* Teahouse in Dushanbe, are venues for wedding parties and destinations for guests on official state visits.

Many people in the West first learned about Asian teahouses from members of the armed forces returning from the Pacific theater of war in World War II or the Korean War. Others became aware of teahouses by watching the film or reading the Pulitzer Prize-winning book *Teahouse of the August Moon* by John Patrick and Vern Sneider. It is the story of villagers in post–World War II Okinawa who preferred to build a teahouse in their village rather than a school, as American advisers, with their very American "can do" attitude, had urged them to do.

Tea Culture

Asians and Middle Easterners take the customs, procedures, and details of tea preparation and drinking very seriously. For example, they derive great pleasure from the color of steaming tea in a small teacup or the design of an engraved silver sugar container. The fact that Iranians and Tajiks believe tea prepared in a charcoal-fired samovar has a more pleasing taste than tea brewed from an electric or kerosene-fired one further demonstrates the level of importance of the aesthetics of tea preparation and consumption in Asia.

There are certain activities and customs that enhance the quality of a teahouse visit. While the décor and ambiance of some teahouses promote solitary, quiet meditation, others have an atmosphere more conducive to social interaction and activity, such as chatting, playing chess, or listening to a poet recite and act out traditional poetry.

People all over Asia visit teahouses to socialize, relax, enjoy their beauty and peace, and drink tea. Here two Tajik women enjoy tea and conversation at an open-air choihona *in Dushanbe, Tajikistan, Boulder's sister city.*

The Cultural Context of the Boulder-Dushanbe Teahouse

In order to understand and appreciate the meaning of Boulder's unique Dushanbe Teahouse, one has to understand the cultural context from which the building sprang.

There are four traditions of Central Asian and Persian cultural history that are relevant to both the form and the function of the *choihona*. They are:

- The Commercial tradition, associated with the *caravanserai* or *khan* (inn) of the ancient Silk Road

- The Meeting-place tradition, associated with the Persian tavern, the *mei-khane* (literally, "wine-house") repeatedly mentioned in the poetry of the great Persian poet Omar Khayyam

- The Spiritual tradition, associated with the most important example of Islamic architectural achievement, the mosque (*masjid*)

- The Aesthetic tradition, associated with the pleasure pavilions of Central Asian potentates, such as Tamerlane, or Kubla Khan

---

The Poetry of Tajik Teahouse Names

The names of Tajik teahouses express the romantic, aesthetic meaning that they hold for Tajiks:

- **Sa'odat** ("Happiness"), in Dushanbe
- **Rohat** ("Comfort"), in Dushanbe (Built in 1958–59 by architects D. D. Gendlin and K. N. Terledkii.)
- **Faroghat** ("Leisure"), in Dushanbe (Built in the 1970's by architects G. V. Salaminod and Sh. Zubaidov.)
- **Panjshanbe** ("Thursday"), in Khujand
- **Orom** ("The Peaceful Place"), in Isfara
- **Guli Surkh** ("Red Flower"), in Urateppe
- **Dilkusho** ("Happy Heart"), in Qurqanteppe
- **Chor-bed** ("Four Willows")

This is the famous "Rohat" Teahouse in Dushanbe. Rohat means "Comfort" or "Relaxation." It is a popular destination for both visitors to the capital of Tajikistan and to city residents.

The Commercial Tradition of Teahouses

It is known that camel caravans crisscrossed Central and Southern Asia for thousands of years, both on the so-called "Silk Road," which passed through what is now Tajikistan, and along its hundreds of tributaries. The "Silk Road" was a network of roads and trails that connected East Asia to the Arab world and to the Mediterranean countries. Marco Polo and other explorers who traveled along the ancient Silk Road were constantly exposed to new ideas, commercial products, sights, sounds and tastes. Some of these cultural artifacts circulated throughout Europe and the Far East and continue to influence life today. Traveling along the Silk Road, like surfing the Internet nowadays, meant encountering unexpected surprises, discoveries and new knowledge. Today the people who live where the Silk Road once existed are heirs to a heritage of trade and cultural exchange that still enriches their lives.

> "At the end of each day's journey, there is a rest house known as a khan where travelers can stay with their animals....They have public wells and shops where people can buy what they need..."
>
> —Arab historian and traveler Ibn Battuta, writing about the road between Cairo and Damascus in 1326[25]

Trade was the reason for the Silk Road's existence, and along with trade came a need for rest stops. While in the early days it was often the custom to knock on a stranger's door to seek room and board, commercial eating-houses and inns began to appear around the 16th century. The *caravanserai*s evolved as the multi-service stations for the merchants who rode in the caravans. They provided a place to sleep, quarter and feed animals, store and display commercial goods, pray, eat, rest, and clean up. Travelers would pass along news from the "outside world" and gather news to take along to their next stops. Some of these rest stops grew to become villages and even cities because of their strategic locations that allowed for access to water, tillable land, and markets. Once the towns created semi-permanent or permanent marketplaces, mosques, schools, and other institutions, teahouses also sprang up as well to provide services not only to long-distance travelers but to town residents. Thus, the *caravanserai* is one of the forerunners of the *choihona*.

Once guarding the ancient "Silk Road," the 17th century Hissar fortress consisted of stronghold gates, two madrasahs (religious schools), a caravanserai, and a stone dome mosque. It is a now major tourist attraction in Tajikistan.

One 17th century French traveler noted that, unlike in European inns, in *caravanserais* "…women were not generally allowed to be seen in public. Correspondingly, eating habits were generally simpler; furniture, apart from carpets, was not required…"[26] Many *caravanserais* still exist in Central Asia and the Middle East, but some of them are in ruin. Some are being superseded by gas stations, fast food restaurants, motels, and modest road-side teahouses serving the modern traveller in cars and buses. Others, such as in Bukhara and Samarkand (in what is now Uzbekistan), have been refurbished and converted to bazaars and tourist sites.

Although men normally frequented Tajik teahouses in the past, more and more women are enjoying them in modern times. While one young Tajik man told me that in his view "it is a place of old men[27]," a Tajik woman told me, "I remember when I was a medical student, my classmates and I often were gathering in Saodat Choihona (It was right across from our medical school), and had lunches and dinners (there). We even organized cultural programs there, such as reading poetry, listening to classical music, watching beautiful Tajik dancing, movies, etc."[28]

Tajiks in national costumes enjoying one of the national pastimes.

The concept of the modern restaurant began in the 16th century when English inns and taverns began to serve one meal a day at a fixed time and price, at a common table, and usually distinguished by a special dish. The word "restaurant" was first used in 1765 for a Paris establishment serving light ("restoring") dishes. The White Horse Tavern in Newport, R.I., (founded 1673) claims to be the oldest American restaurant.[29] In Boulder, The Trident Cafe and Penny Lane on Pearl Street and the Brewing Market on 13th Street are the three oldest coffee-houses in Boulder.

The Meeting Place Tradition of Teahouses

The company one finds in a teahouse also has a bearing on the teahouse experience. Regulars like to see friends with whom they converse, play games such as chess and backgammon, share a water pipe, and enjoy camaraderie and the ambiance of the teahouse. Some have been performance venues for storytellers, since there were no written materials for ordinary people, and the fables, legends, morality tales, etc. were recited in the teahouses in order to pass along cultural history in an oral form to younger generations.

The *choihona*'s ancestor in this social context is the *mei-khane* (wine-house). *Mei-khane* is the Persian word that the many translators and re-writers of Omar Khayyam's quatrains turned into "tavern." For example, Boulder artist Aprylisa Snyder chose to include Edward Fitzgerald's translation of Khayyam's famous quatrain in her attractive creek-side walkway art on the south side of the Boulder Teahouse:

> **A European Traveler Comments on a 17th Century Persian Wine-house**
>
> "A leisurely form of amusement was found in the cabarets, particularly in certain districts (in Isfahan).... People met there to drink cordials, liqueurs or coffee, to smoke tobacco or opium during the day or in the cool of the evenings, chat or listen to poetry. These palaces were full of animation and entertainment and appealed to Persians of all classes with their wide range of amusing, serious, and obscene activities. 'These palaces have large, spacious high-ceilinged rooms of different shapes and are usually located in the most attractive parts of town, because they are the meeting places and the entertainment centers for all the inhabitants."[30]

> *And, as the Cock crew, those who stood before*
> *The Tavern shouted—-"Open then the Door!*
> *"You know how little while we have to stay,*
> *"And, once departed, may return no more."*

The tavern was a symbol of the world, or life, for Khayyam.

During the early days of Soviet rule in Central Asia, there were "Red Teahouses" in Tajikistan. The Soviets established them as "propaganda" centers with special organizational and administrative tasks. The Soviets held Communist Party committee meetings and informal secret meetings in them. To better serve their clientele, the teahouses were given permission to provide newspapers, journals, radios, and chess and backgammon boards for the workers who visited them, as a kind of "perk."

Teahouses later became popular meeting places for war veterans, workers, parliamentarians, scientists, artists, and poets. During the 1970s and 1980s, in major cities like Dushanbe and Khujand, the tradition of building teahouses was revived and several teahouses were constructed.[31]

Photo courtesy of the Daily Camera

Customers of Boulder's Trident Booksellers and Café on Pearl Street keep the coffeehouse meeting-place tradition alive. Like Dushanbe, Boulder is known for its many cafes where locals meet to share a cup of tea or coffee.

The Spiritual Aspect of Teahouses

Many visitors to the Boulder *Choihona* report experiencing something of a spiritual feeling there. With the exception of the busy lunch and dinner hours, the ambiance at the Boulder-Dushanbe Teahouse is serene and conducive to meditation and rest. This can be attributed to the decor, much of which embodies spiritual values and symbols found in Central Asian and Middle Eastern religious buildings, including:

> "*Your eyes are drawn upward (in the Teahouse). Perhaps that has some spiritual significance.*"
> —Former Boulder-Dushanbe Sister Cities President Mary Axe.

- Ceramic tiles, carved woodwork, central pools, and vegetal motifs (perhaps most commonly associated with mosque decorations—in the Islamic tradition the vegetal motifs of the Teahouse ceiling, pillars, and wall art suggest the gardens of paradise)

- The numerous prayer arches (*mihrab*) found in the ceiling coffers, carved plaster panels, and exterior ceramic panels

- The Arabic inscription "Allah Akbar" ("God is Great") painted on first West-facing cross beam to the left of the entrance as one enters the room

In this text on Persian mosques, the late distinguished Persian art professor Arthur Upham Pope could have just as easily been discussing Central Asian teahouses:

> "We can understand how the Persian mosque assumed its familiar aspect, the wide court, the groves of pillars, the pool and watercourses, the kiosk-like *ivans*, the twining flowery arabesque decorations, and, above all, the color—for Persian architecture is the only architecture man has developed where color plays an equal part with form. Persia alone could make the carpet a serious form of art—it is the simulacrum of a garden, and for the Persian therefore an image of the world."[32]

Middle Eastern and Central Asian architecture and art owe its greatness to the rise of Islam, which began in the 7th century A.D. This is the Mausoleum of Ismail the Samanid in Bukhara, Uzbekistan. It is canopy tomb, a domed cube open on four sides. The Samanids ruled Central Asia from 891-1005.

The Aesthetic Tradition of Teahouses

Another reason Asians visit teahouses is to enjoy the beauty of their architecture, furnishings, art, and ambiance. The room's interior design, serving dishes, staff, furniture, carpets, paintings and other art provide a visual experience that sets the mood for quiet contemplation or convivial conversation.

One example of a pleasure palace was the Ali Qapu in Isfahan. Shah Abbas the Great, who ruled Persia from 1588-1629, would sit on his second-story porch and watch polo being played in the grand square below him. At other times he listened to music in the mirrored music room or lounged in his chambers admiring the many scenes that were painted directly onto the walls.

In Xanadu did Kubla Khan
A stately pleasure-dome decree:
Where Alph, the sacred river, ran
Through caverns measureless to man
Down to a sunless sea.
So twice five miles of fertile ground
With walls and towers were girdled round:
And there were gardens bright with sinuous rills,
Where blossomed many an incense-bearing tree;
And here were forests ancient as the hills,
Enfolding sunny spots of greenery.

—Samuel Taylor Coleridge: "Kubla Khan or, a Vision in a Dream: A Fragment"

Photo courtesy of Emily Wells Gianfortoni

I visited one teahouse in Isfahan (Iran) in which the ambiance owed much to the enormous antique brass samovar that sat opposite the main entrance of the hall like an obese sultan on his throne. Another I visited was prized for its display of religious paintings and well-known religious story tellers. Yet another, in Turkey, was famous for its extraordinary garden. And one in a mountain village in southern Iran is known for its collection of carpets (a catalog of local tribal production).

In both Turkic Central Asian and Persian histories, the *khans* (tribal chieftains), *shahs* (kings), and *emirs* (princes) have had a well-documented tradition of pleasure-seeking. It was often the custom of the royals and their friends to indulge themselves to extremes in the sensual pleasures of art, architecture, gardens, poetry, sport, food, drink, women, and other merriment. They often erected grand buildings, tents, pavilions, garden kiosks, and other structures in which to provide a venue for their pastimes. These structures were designed by the *creme de la creme* of architects and contained the best quality textiles, paintings, and appointments.

No mention of pleasure palaces should be made without a reference to Tamerlane (Teymour), who ruled Central Asia with an iron fist from, living from 1336-1405. Unlike Shah Abbas, Tamerlane had a nomadic tribal background, so he preferred to pass the time in tents, some of which were as large as a palace and were furnished in a palatial manner.

Tamerlane, a son of a lesser tribal chieftain, was born in 1336 at Kesh, about fifty miles south of Samarkand in present day Uzbekistan (an area claimed by some Tajiks). Tamerlane was a dedicated patron of the arts, a role he pursued with terrifying determination. Taking care to protect craftsmen and teachers from the armies he sent to plunder foreign cities, Tamerlane's typical practice was to herd captured artisans back to Samarkand to beautify his capital architecturally and adorn it with fine paintings, books, elegant metal and woodwork, and other exotica. Above all, he was a superb, ruthless and highly ambitious soldier.

The gardens around his palace were one and a half to two square miles in area. On the east side was the *Bagh-i-Dilkusha*, "the garden that cheers the heart," joined on to the town by a long avenue. But the favorite place of all, which its owner called his hermitage, was *Bagh-i-Bhisht*, "the Paradise Garden."

Since the Boulder *Choihona* could be classified as a garden pavilion, at least in its original design, it is worthwhile to look at the fact that Tamerlane often constructed garden pavilions and tents in and around his many gardens. "Timurids [Tamerlane and his successors] continued the practice of their predecessors of entertaining important guests and foreign envoys in their gardens. Ceremonial surrounding events, such as weddings or investitures, required an outdoor setting. Such occasions still took place in magnificent tents, pitched in the open meadow, but, alternatively, the formal garden and pavilion could provide a substitute."[33]

This Persian miniature painting from the 15th century depicts Tamerlane being entertained under a garden pavilion near Samarkand, in what is today Uzbekistan.

First-Person Account of Drinking Tea in a Central Asian Teahouse

It comes as no surprise that it is an Englishman, Robin Magowan, who poetically describes the pleasures of drinking tea in a Central Asian choihona in Bukhara, Uzbekistan:

"Drinking tea in such circumstance can't help but be a form of meditation. In the first place the tea comes so scalding there is no way for even the thirstiest to gulp it down. You have to proceed slowly, as if it were a hot towel, not a cup, that you are drawing to your face, letting each sip adjust you that much more fully to the light, the heat, and those in their caftans and turbans and vests around you.

"By now the tea is drinking you more than you are drinking it. Water, always so precious—life itself, those around you might say—is coursing through your veins. You feel yourself spreading out to meet its flow, becoming one with your sleeves, and all of the life circulating around you... Here among the trees and the heat and the piercing music, conversation may be too difficult to attempt....

"The bed table you are sitting on is a real bed, if bigger than those we tend to sleep on-a bed for six....You don't squat as much as sprawl Roman-fashion, leaning back on your elbows and letting a leg jut out. Suspended on this kind of flying carpet, you find the exchanges can begin to happen in a way they don't when you are seated face-to-face in chairs, legs solidly planted on the ground. Who you are...is less important than the visual space, the ongoing picture, you create between you."[34]

Photo courtesy of Roger Kova

Taom va choi

CHAPTER 4

Food and Tea

"The first cup caresses my dry lips and throat,
The second shatters the walls of my lonely sadness,
The third searches the dry rivulets of my soul to find the stories of five thousand scrolls.
With the fourth the paint of past injustice vanishes through my pores.
The fifth purifies my flesh and bone.
With the sixth I am in touch with the immortals.
The seventh gives such pleasure I can hardly bear.
The fresh wind blows through my wings
As I make my way to Penglai."

—LU TONG, TANG DYNASTY (A.D. 618-907)

Teahouses exist, foremost, as places to drink tea. Drinking tea is one of life's simple pleasures that billions of people indulge in regularly. Tea is enjoyed equally by both aristocrats and taxi-drivers. The reason for its popularity may be its taste. Or it may be its caffeine, the most widely used psychoactive substance in the world. The most notable behavioral effects of caffeine—increased alertness, energy, and ability to concentrate—normally occur after drinking a small cup of tea.

The popularity of tea-drinking could also be due to its social aspects. Historian Woodruff D. Smith wrote: "Apparently, coffee and tea possess public value because, when taken by people in company under the appropriate circumstances, they encourage imbibers to behave in a desirable way (to do business, hold conversation, and act, or at least speak, intelligently) and not to behave in undesirable ways…"[35]

he Tajik national
sh, plov (pilaf)

I once watched the late Tajik Teahouse woodcarver Mirpulat Mirakhmatov break his Ramadan fast while in Boulder with a simple cup of green tea. I will never forget the way he savored the tea he had poured from his thermos in Boulder's Ebin Fine Park after a day of hard work at the Teahouse construction site. I will never forget how the tea brought a smile of contentment to his face. That day at dusk, in January, 1998, Mirpulat helped me understand the meaning of tea.

Tajiks drink tea out of a *piyola*, a small bowl often decorated with a cotton plant motif. Teapots often have similar designs. The person pouring the tea customarily places his hand over his heart when handing the cup to others at the table.

Photo courtesy of Mary Hey

A Tajik villager enjoys a refreshing cup of choi *in the mountain air.*

The tea plant is *camellia sinensis*, a native of Southeast Asia. The tea brewed from its leaves has probably been drunk in China and nearby countries (Tajikistan shares a border with China) for thousands of years. Arab traders who explored China learned about tea by 900 A.D., but the first references to tea by Europeans came more than 600 years later in 1559.[36] England became the first Western tea-drinking country in the 17th century after travelers brought the concept of boiling tealeaves and drinking it for pleasure home with them from Asia. In Asia itself, the influence from China spread to all regions as did the Chinese name for the drink, *cha*. While in Central and East Asia green tea is usually drunk, Iranians and Indians normally drink black tea.

Interesting Facts about Tea

- Many Tajiks insist that a cup of hot green tea is the best antidote to the oppressive summer heat.

- Tea is the world's second most popular drink in the world (after water).[37]

- The English in the 18th century called the establishment where they drank tea a "coffee-house"; so do the Iranians in the present day.

- The word for "tea" in most Asian, Semitic, and eastern European languages is a close variation of the Chinese word *cha.*

- Thomas Sullivan, of New York, was looking for a cheaper way to distribute tea when he came up with the idea of packaging leaves in little silk bags. And the tea bag was born in 1904.[38]

- A search for "tea" in Google.com rendered 16.2 million Web pages, while "beer" rendered only 12.6 million. "Coffee," however, tallied a whopping 24.8 million pages.

- "Room puppets" were expensive toys of feudal lords and influential merchants in the 18th century in Japan. The tea-serving doll was designed to bring tea to an amazed guest. It was used more as a ploy to break the ice and get the conversation going, rather than to actually serve tea. The host placed a tea cup on the tray held by the doll, which activated its mechanism to move it forward. It stopped when the guest picked up the tea cup, lifting the weight from the tray. When the cup was placed back on the tray, the doll turned around and walked back to its original position.[39]

- Compressed tea—also known as brick tea— is found mainly in the south of China and is the oldest form of tea made in China. It is still used by some tribes in the southern part of China as a form of medication or Shaman magic. It is made by high pressure compression into shapes resembling bricks.[40]

- In the early American Colonies, tea leaves were boiled at length, creating a bitter concoction. Then the leaves were salted and eaten with butter.[41]

Green Tea, Black Tea

The difference between green and black tea is in the processing of the tea leaves. When leaves are dried immediately and completely they produce green tea. When the leaves are only partially dried and then allowed to ferment, various types of black teas are produced, including orange pekoe and *souchong*. *Oolong* tea is produced by only allowing the fermentation to proceed a certain amount. All teas contain

Boulder Dushanbe Teahouse Specialty Green Teas

Of the more than 100 teas served by the Boulder Choihona's, these are its speciality teas:

• **Boulder Breakfast Black Tea**— exclusively blended for the Teahouse, this is a blend of Keemun, Assam, and Yunnan full leaf teas. It has a clear, crisp, bright cup that is great with milk.

• **Boulder Tangerine Herbal Tea**—brewed exclusively by Celestial Seasonings for the *Choihona*.

• **Friendship Tea**—A flavored black tea blended by Sara Martinelli as a fund-raising specialty tea.

• **Jade Spring**—This green tea has been chosen as our house tea because of its rich, nutty flavor without a hint of bitterness. This tea is a wonderful tea from China with a beautiful leaf style.

• **Snow Blossom**—An exclusive house blend of green tea and the petals of chamomile, rose, jasmine, and lavender.

Even before the Teahouse was built, Boulder had a strong "tea presence." Boulder is home to Celestial Seasonings (www.celestialseasonings.com), the world's largest distributor of tea products. Its free 45-minute tours and tastings at 4600 Sleepytime Drive in northeast Boulder, like the Boulder Dushanbe Teahouse, is a major Boulder tourist attraction. Boulder is also home to the Herb Research Foundation, a clearinghouse for herb-related subjects. Photo courtesy of Celestial Seasonings caffeine, but green tea has about one-third less caffeine than black tea. Interestingly, Tajiks call their green tea "blue" tea (*choi kabut*). Tajiks drink both green and black tea. A special type of green tea Tajiks serve to honored guests is called *gulchoi* (literally, "flower-tea"). In this rarer and thus more expensive variety, the tea leaves are cut from the plant before they are fully opened, so the tea has an exceptionally pleasant taste and fragrance.[42]

The four main types of green tea[43] are:
- *Gunpowder tea*: Grown in China and Taiwan, this tea has a clear yellow-green color and a slightly bitter-sweet taste. It is easily recognized by its round, pellet shape.

- *Hyson tea*: This is pan-fried green tea with a fragrant, bitter taste.

- *Jasmine tea*: This is a blend of Chinese green teas and white jasmine flowers to produce a light subtle taste with a mild, sweet flavor.

- *Sencha*: This is a green tea grown in Japan and the most common of Japanese tea exports.

Then What is "Chai"?

In Tajiki, "*choi*" means tea. In Iran, tea is called "*chai*". The "*chai*" that has entered the English language in the past 15 years or so is a mixture of black teas, milk, sugar, honey, and various spices. The types of tea and the spices vary by region and culture although typically, cardamom, ginger, and even pepper are the most common. *Chai* is an ancient beverage savored for its rich and complex varieties.

Both green and black teas have gained popularity in the West in the past two decades partially because of marketing efforts of such companies as Boulder's Celestial Seasonings. Celestial Seasonings has popularized herbal teas (not true teas because they actually contain no tea). Some of their most popular flavors include lemon grass, peppermint, hibiscus, and chamomile. Celestial Seasonings also created a special tea blend just for the Boulder-Dushanbe Teahouse—Boulder Tangerine.

Tajik Food

It is interesting to note that there are very few restaurants in Dushanbe. In general people don't eat outside of their homes for both economic and cultural reasons. However, when they do, they often go to teahouses.

The most popular *choihona* in Dushanbe is the *Rohat Choihona* (*rohat* means "comfort" or "relaxation"). It is located in downtown Dushanbe near the parliament building on Shohidi square. Another popular eating place is the *Saodat* (which means "Abode of Felicity") *Choihona*.

A Tajik chef prepares kabob in front of the Saodat Teahouse in Dushanbe.

The most commonly eaten dish in Tajikistan is *plov*, a rich pilaf with meat, steamed carrots and peas. *Plov*, which is served at the Teahouse, is considered the national dish and it is eaten frequently at parties, in restaurants, and at home. Tajiks are extremely proud of their national dish, as they are of their fruits, including grapes, apricots, apples, melons, pomegranates, and pears.

Other popular Tajik foods include
• *mantu* (steamed stuffed noodles)
• *oshi ugro* (noodle soup)
• *shish-kabobs*
• *mastoba* (rice soup)
• *shavla* (thin rice porridge cooked with oil, onions, carrots, and meat)
• *tushbera* (soup)
• *katlama* (rich flat cake, fried in oil)
• *shurbo bo gushti gusfand* (mutton soup)

Tajiks often have bread with honey and cream as light snacks. One kind of bread popular among Tajiks is *nan*, a flatbread baked in a clay *tandoori* oven.

Tajik/Persian Food at the Boulder Teahouse

Although the "traditional world ethnic cuisine" menu at the Boulder-Dushanbe Teahouse changes regularly, proprietor Lenny Martinelli tries to always include a few entrees from Central Asia and the Middle East. *Plov* (Tajik pilaf) is also usually on the menu. Another popular menu item is *khoresht-e bademjan*, a scrumptious eggplant stew. Central Asians and Middle Easterners do about as many interesting things with an eggplant as Mexicans do with chile. They stew, stuff, bake, fry, roast, and pickle it. And, as aficionados of deli cuisine know, smashing eggplant into a paste with garlic and olive oil to produce *baba ganouj* is a favorite use.

Other popular Persian-Tajik dishes sometimes found on the Boulder-Dushanbe *Choihona*'s menu are *khoresht-e fesenjan*, a stewed chicken dish with a sauce made from pomegranate sauce, crushed walnuts, onions, and spices, and Persian lamb kabob.

Photo courtesy of Sara Martinelli

Boulder-Dushanbe Teahouse proprietor Lenny Martinelli gives a tour to visiting students. He is wearing a traditional Tajik chapan *robe.*

Navruz *means "New Day", the annual celebration of the Persian New Year, which falls on the first day of spring. The Boulder Teahouse hosts an annual* Navruz *party. Here three Tajik girls dance at the 2002* Navruz *festival. The dances of Central Asia are noted for their dramatic facial expressions, expressive hand gestures, lyrical movements and dizzying spins. The costumes are made from atlas* Silk *(ikat) .*

A Conversation with a Tajik about Blue Tea

Firuz Saidovich, a Dushanbe native who onced live in Boulder, discusses tea and tea-drinking in Tajikistan.

Question: What kind of tea do Tajiks drink?
Firuz: 75% of the people drink green tea, which for some reason is called "Blue Tea", or *choi kabut* in Tajiki, and about 25% drink black tea.

Question: Does just about everyone drink it then?
Firuz: Yes, in general the older the person, the more they drink, and the stronger they like it. My grandmother drinks at least 5 liters a day, for example.

Question: What do they put in it?
Firuz: Usually nothing. Once in a while some people add some sugar, but only in the morning.

Question: Why is it so popular?
Firuz: I don't know. I think it's kind of like an addiction. It builds up your feeling and calms you down.

Question: How do you make it? Do you use a samovar?
Firuz: Never. That's a Russian thing. First you boil water for seven minutes. It must be really hot. Then you rinse out a ceramic teapot with the boiling water to warm the pot. Then you put in a handful of tealeaves and fill the pot up with boiling water. Then after you let it sit for a few minutes, you drink it. It must be really hot!

Question: What do you use to drink it?
Firuz: It's actually a shallow cup called a piyola. I think they have some at the Boulder Teahouse. Frankly, I really wish they would use those instead of the American cups, or at least have them available.

Question: Do you offer tea when guests visit?
Firuz: Oh, yes. When someone comes to visit my grandmother, that's the first thing they get.

Question: So she fixes it for them?
Firuz: No, if it's an older person, my father does. If it's a younger person, it's my job. That is one way we show respect for the grandmother.

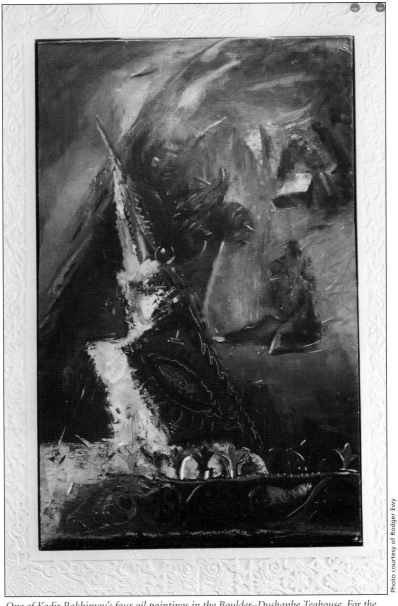

One of Kodir Rakhimov's four oil paintings in the Boulder–Dushanbe Teahouse. For the most part, the paintings have food and sea themes.

CHAPTER 5

Tajikistan and the Tajik People

"On my most recent trip to Tajikistan I conducted 42 interviews with people I considered competent to evaluate the question, "Why did Tajikistan not fall back into war after the peace agreement?" I was frankly surprised at the common response, "Tajiks are peaceful people."

—AMERICAN RESEARCHER JONATHAN ZARTMAN

Dushanbe

Boulder's Tajik sister city is an attractive metropolis with wide, tree-lined boulevards, and a mix of European-style and traditional Central Asian buildings, shops, Soviet-style apartment blocks, parks, teahouses, and cultural monuments. Around town you see open-air bazaars, crowds rushing to shops and work, and ubiquitous traffic jams. Dushanbe is located in the wide Varzob River valley beneath the snow-capped mountains of the Hissar Range.

Tajikistan is a beautiful country embracing the ancient Silk Road. To the east the majestic Pamir Mountains separate it from China. The former Soviet republics of Kyrgyzstan and Uzbekistan lie to the north and west respectively. Afghanistan is to the south. Dushanbe, located in the western part of the nation, is the capital of Tajikistan. It is approximately 200 miles north of Kabul, Afghanistan.

Dushanbe means "Monday." Records show that as early as 1676, on each Monday of the week, villagers from the surrounding areas brought their produce to market at this spot. Nowadays Dushanbe struggles to modernize and to keep up with its burgeoning population and deteriorating socio-economic conditions, the result of a decade of instability following Tajikistan's independence from the Soviet Union in 1991. However, there are reasons to be optimistic about the future of the country (see p. 93).

Tajik school children in one of Dushanbe's schools. Tajikistan has a literacy rate of over 99%. (right) Tajik schoolchildren enjoying an outing.

Photos courtesy of Roger Kovacs

Quick Facts about Dushanbe

- Capital of Tajikistan

- On the banks of the Dushanbinka River

- 2,475 feet above sea level

- About 100 miles from the Afghani border

- From 1929–1961, was called Stalinabad

- The Republic's largest industrial center

- A population of over 600,000

- Home of numerous institutions of higher education, including Tajikistan State University, State Pedagogical University, State Medical University, State Polytechnic University, State Agricultural University, Shevchenko Pedagogical Institute, The Academy of Sciences of Tajikistan, Slavonic University, and The Technological University

- Home of Ferdowsi National Library, the Aini Theater for Opera and Ballet and the Tajik Philharmonic Society

Photo courtesy of The CIA World Factbook of Tajikistan

Map of Tajikistan

Tajikistan

Tajikistan is about the size of the Colorado plains east of the Front Range of the Rocky Mountains, but its topography is more like that of the western part of the state. It is nearly all (93%) mountainous, with several peaks rising well above 20,000 feet. The highest peaks in the country are Ismoili Somoni Peak (24,590 feet), which was formerly called Communism Peak, Garmo Peak, Stalin Peak (24,590 feet), and Lenin Peak, formerly called Kaufmann Peak (23,405 feet). As in Colorado, gushing rivers come down to the dry plains. The Tajik climate has often been compared to that of New Mexico—dry and hot in the summer, dry and cold in the winter.

The southeastern part of Tajikistan is an arid plateau from 12,000 to 15,000 feet high. The only extensive low districts are

Mountains in the Mastchoh region of the Zarafshon valley of the Sogd region of Tajikistan.
Photo courtesy of Nazir Sharipov

the Tajik section of the Fergana Valley in the north and the hot, dry Hissar and Vakhsh valleys in the southwest. The Amu Darya, Syr Darya, and Zeravshan are the chief rivers and are used for irrigation. Additional dams and irrigation projects, notably the Great Gissar Canal, have opened almost 1 million acres (400,000 hectares) of land to cultivation.

Tajikistan's population is more than 6 million. Most of Tajikistan's people are concentrated in its narrow, deep intermountain valleys. About 65% of the population is composed of Tajiks (also spelled Tadjiks or Tadzhiks), a Sunni Muslim people who speak a language akin to the Farsi of Iran and Dari of Afghanistan. In addition to the capital of Dushanbe, other important cities are Khujand (where the wood of the Boulder Teahouse was carved), Uroteppa, and Qurghonteppa.

In the Pamir Ran, northwest Tajiki, Somoni Peak, called Peak Commu, and Stalin Peak, to 24,590 ft (7,495 the highest poi, Tajikistan and i, former USSR as we, the right half o, photo is the Boro, But,
Photo by Hartmut Bie

Quick Facts about Tajikistan*

Population 6,863,752 (July 2003 est.)

Ethnicity Tajik 64.9%, Uzbek 25%, Russian 3.5%, other 6.6%

Topography 93% mountainous

Highest peak Ismoili Somoni Peak: 24,590 feet

Industries Mining, machine tools, cotton milling

Agriculture Cotton, maize, fruit, sheep, silkworms

Languages Tajik, Russian

Natural Resources Hydropower, some petroleum, uranium, mercury, brown coal, lead, zinc, antimony, tungsten, silver, gold, precious stones

Religions Sunni Muslim 80%, Shi'a Muslim (especially Isma'ili) 5%

Population Growth Rate 2.13% (2003 est.)

Birth Rate 32.78 births/1,000 population (2003 est.)

Infant Mortality Rate 113.43 deaths/1,000 live births

Life Expectancy at Birth total population: 64.37 years; male: 61.39 years; female: 67.5 years (2003 est.)

Literacy 99.4%

Independence September 9, 1991 (from Soviet Union)

Currency Tajikistani somoni: 2.7 per US dollar (2002)

Chief of State President Emomali Rahmonov

Adapted from the CIA World Factbook on Tajikistan (2003)

Early History of Tajikistan

The current Tajik Republic harkens back to the Samanid Dynasty (875-999), which, centered on Bukhara, ruled what is now Tajikistan, as well as territory to the south and west. The Samanids supported the revival of the written Persian language in the wake of the Arab Islamic conquest in the early 8th century. They played an important role in preserving the culture of the pre-Islamic Persian-speaking world. The Samanids were the last Persian-speaking dynasty to rule Central Asia.

The Samanid Dynasty, which paid tribute to the Abbasid Caliph in Baghdad, lasted only about 200 years from 819-992. It was a source of Persian inspiration for the Islamic world. It was also the source of support for many of the early Islamic poets, scientists, and artists. Arguably, without the Samanid influence, later developments in Persian culture would have not taken place. The current Tajik government embraces the Samanids as a cultural symbol of Tajik civilization.

A 1600-year-old 50´ statue of a sleeping Buddha is on display at the Tajikistan's Museum of National Antiquities in Dushanbe. After Afghanistan's Taliban destroyed the largest Buddhas in Central Asia, the Tajikistan Buddha is the largest ancient Buddha statue in Central Asia. It was first excavated by Soviet archeologists in 1966 from a Buddhist monastery in Ajina Tepa in southern Tajikistan.

Photo courtesy of Scott Raderstorf

The Tajik territory was conquered by the Mongols in the 13th century. In the 16th century, it became part of the Khanate of Bukhara. In the 1890's, the Tajiks were divided into two distinct groups: The Tajiks of the Russian Empire and the Tajiks of Afghanistan. In 1924, the Tajiks of the Russian Empire were Sovietized.

Although the magnificent cities of Samarkand and Bukhara are located in present-day Uzbekistan, they are claimed by both the Tajiks and the Uzbeks as part of their historical heritages. The two cities, which served as major centers of trade and enlightenment on the crossroads of "the Silk Road," are considered showcases of Islamic architecture.

Important Tajik Contributions to World Culture

Tajikistan is heir to a highly developed cultural tradition. In that capacity, it has given the world many outstanding scientists and poets, including:

- **Al-Khwarazmi,** the 9th century mathematician and astronomer who gave his name to algorithms. The title of another of his mathematical works, Al-Jabr, has entered the English language as "algebra."
- **Maulana Jalal al-Din Rumi,** also referred to as Molavi (1207-1273), the greatest Sufi poet of the Persian language, is famous for his didactic epic Masnavi-ye Ma'navi ("Spiritual Couplets"), a work that has widely influenced Muslim mystical thought and literature.
- **Ibn-Sina,** the physician and enlightener of the 10-11th centuries, known in the West as Avicenna.
- **Abu Abdullah Rudaki,** court poet in Bukhara during the Samanid era, is recognized as the "father" of Persian/Tajik literature. One of the main boulevards of Dushanbe is named after this poet. The proposed Cyber Café will be built on this beautiful thoroughfare.
- **Al-Biruni,** the world's foremost astronomer in the 11th century, knew that the earth rotated and that it circled the sun. He also produced the world's finest encyclopedia.
- Tajiks also venerate **Firdowsi,** a poet and composer of the *Shah-nameh (Book of Kings),* the Persian national epic, and Omar Khayyam, of *Rubaiyyat* fame, both born in present-day Iran before the breakup of the Iranian kulturbund.

The Tajiks under the Soviets

The Russians conquered Central Asia, including the region of present-day Tajikistan, in 1868. Thereafter, Bukhara, the center of Tajik culture, was nominally ruled by an Amir of the Manghit family. The Tajiks as a people, however, remained split among several administrative-political entities. The territory, being economically backward, became a source of raw materials. In the aftermath of the 1917 Russian Revolution, Tajikistan became the center of the Basmachi movement, a Muslim anti-Soviet movement that aimed at the restoration of Muslim identity and power in the region.

The movement was crushed by the Red Army in the early 1920's. In 1924, Soviet Tajiks were given an autonomous republic within Uzbekistan; in 1929, Tajikistan became a constituent republic of the USSR.

In December 1990, the Tajikistan parliament passed a resolution of sovereignty. The Republic of Tajikistan declared its independence in September 1991, and in December it joined the Commonwealth of Independent States. When the acting president sought to suspend the country's Communist party, the Communist-led parliament replaced him. The former Communist Party chief, Rakhmon Nabiyev, was elected president in November 1991.

In 1992, Nabiyev was deposed by opposition militias. An ethnically-based civil war quickly erupted. Forces allied with the former Nabiyev government, aided by Russian and Uzbek contingents, retook the capital and most of the country. The parliament abolished the

Two Tajiks office of the president and elected Russian-supported Emomali Rakhmonov as the Head of the Supreme Soviet. After the office of the president was reinstated in 1994, Rahmonov was elected President of the Republic.

Photo courtesy of Roger Kovacs

Tajikistan Today

With much hope for its future, Tajikistan is a country overcoming many problems with a strong and determined people. The good news is that civil conflicts have been mostly resolved and the risk of resumption of the civil war is relatively low. Non-Government Organizations are monitoring elections and educating the population on the process of building a civil society. What they lack in economic resources, Tajikistan's people make up for in hard work and resourcefulness.

While sitting outside the Boulder teahouse next to a gushing clear creek, enjoying lunch and the peace of the day, and looking out at a bustling Saturday morning Farmers Market, it is difficult to imagine the desperate situation that confronts the residents of Boulder's sister city, and even worse, those who live in the Tajik countryside.

Any visitor who has been to Tajikistan and walked through its markets and villages understands a simple truth. Tajikistan is a country with a host of problems and countless wonderful, strong people who are masters at making the best of a difficult situation. However, they need resources to make their dreams come true—dreams of national development, civil society, and a bright future for their children.

The Norak (Nurek) Dam

Tajikistan is a world leader of hydroelectric power and may parlay that resource with its other major exportable asset water to build its future. Its 2,700 megawatt Norak hydroelectric plant on the Vakhsh River to the east of Dushanbe is one of the largest power-producing dams in the world and is said to be the highest dam in the world at 1000 feet above sea level. Tajikistan ranks eighth in the world in the production of hydroelectric power. It is constructing an even larger and higher dam, Rogunsk, that will allow it to export power to Afghanistan, Pakistan and China. Tajikistan also has promising deposits of gold, silver and aluminum. It now produces 350,000 tons of aluminum a year.

Tajikistan Dossier: The Sad, Recent History of Independent Tajikistan

Item: Following the collapse of the USSR in 1991, Tajikistan's first few years were marred by violence and turbulence. It was dealt a severe blow by the loss of its traditional markets. Independence deprived the country of much-needed Soviet subsidies, foodstuffs and aid, a loss it is still reeling from today.

Item: Within nine months of independence, a bloody five-year civil war broke out, ultimately taking some 60,000 lives, while threatening to divide the nation along regional lines.

Item: A drought in 2000-2001 left many households more vulnerable than ever before, and prompted a major upsurge in labor migration, particularly to Russia. As a result, at least one in four families has a member working abroad.

Item: The civil war devastated the country's economy and infrastructure, particularly in the rural areas. Free of debt at independence, Tajikistan subsequently accumulated $1 billion worth of external liabilities, equivalent to 100 percent of its GDP.

Item: Nearly 20 percent of the country's schools were destroyed during the civil war, while the rest fell into disrepair. Health care and other social services plummeted.

Item: Nowadays grinding poverty has become, without a doubt, the primary challenge facing Tajiks, with unemployment estimated to be over 30 percent.

Item: "Fifty percent of the country's population – or some 3 million people – are dependent on the remittances sent back to them from family members working abroad," Muzafar Zaripov, a program officer and focal point for labor migration for IOM, told IRIN in Dushanbe.

Item: According to the UN, Tajikistan grows only 40 percent of its cereal needs. Lack of access to food and productive resources, including land, seeds and water, remains the root cause of the problem. Food security for the poorest strata of the population, numbering about 300,000, remains fragile.

Item: Anne Pater, the head of the mission in Dushanbe for the international NGO Action Against Hunger concurred, in 2003 drew attention to the plight of children. "Close to 350,000 children under the age of five in Tajikistan are chronically malnourished. This is a major source of concern," she said.

Item: Compounding the problem are recent (2003) recurrent outbreaks of infectious diseases such as typhoid, measles, anthrax, brucellosis and Congo-Crimea hemorrhagic fever, which regularly overwhelmed medical capacities, according to this year's UN consolidated appeals process (CAP) for the country.

Item: Vivax malaria was recently endemic in many parts of Tajikistan, and the WHO estimates that 400,000 new cases of infection occurred in 2002, while increasing levels of falciparum malaria and resistance to anti-malaria drugs are of particular concern.

Item: Tuberculosis is also on the rise. Official statistics show an increase in cases from 32 per 100,000 in 1996 to 64 per 100,000 people in 2002.

Tajikistan Dossier: And Some Good News

Item: Tajikistan's five-year civil war formally ended with the signing of the General Agreement on the Establishment of Peace and National Accord in June 1997. Subsequently the country launched a continuous process of national reconciliation and dialogue to restore peace, stability and security.

Item: As part of the peace agreement, former members of the United Tajik Opposition were included in government structures. The Islamic Renaissance Party of Tajikistan, one of the major political actors in the conflict, was not only legally recognized but gained two seats in the national parliament in the elections of 2000.

Item: The ICG report said the country's experience in ending the civil war and integrating opposition factions into government had won deserved praise, noting recent improved security and stability country-wide over the past two years as a result.

Item: Today, (2004) political pluralism in Tajikistan is slowly gaining pace: there are already six registered political parties contributing toward the creation of peaceful dialogue and debate, and such internal mechanisms as would strengthen the irreversibility of the peace process.

Item: The Tajik people are now enjoying enhanced political stability and security despite the fact there are several factors - both internal and external - that could adversely affect the existing situation.

Item: Given certain internal improvements, Tajikistan requires less humanitarian, and more development, assistance. That gradual progress towards stability and development is being made is undeniable. Over the past two years, the atmosphere, particularly in the urban areas, has become more positive.

Item: Economic conditions, too, are improving. There has been a growth rate of between 9 percent and 10 percent from 1998-2003 with at least one-third of the growth coming from non-traditional sectors - mainly services and trade. Experts say that there has also been growth in small-scale agriculture.

Item: Generally speaking, an important stage in the reform process towards achieving macro-economic stability coupled with high growth and much lower inflation has been completed. However, this remains an area requiring more work if the positive trend is to be sustained.

Item: Whereas donor response to Tajikistan has been strong, the government must now work to ensure that donor funds are well spent. In May 2003, the Consultative Group, a forum of all donors organized by the World Bank, pledged around $1 billion for Tajikistan over the next three years (2003-2005), one-quarter of which would be in the form of grants.

Item: What is apparent, meanwhile, is that Tajikistan is at a crossroads for change, requiring a government open to change and a donor community willing to support it in effecting change. The question is whether both parties are fully ready for the task at hand.

(This information about Tajikistan is provided courtesy of the "Asia-English" Service of the Integrated Regional Information Networks (IRIN), part of the United Nations Office for the Coordination of Humanitarian Affairs (OCHA) http://www.irinnews.org.)

The Tajiks

The largest ethnic group in Tajikistan is the Tajik. It numbers an estimated 3.5 million, out of a total population of about 6.8 million. The Tajiks are descendants of ethnic Iranians.

The next largest group in Tajikistan is the Uzbek, a Turkic race that originally was nomadic. The Uzbeks migrated to Central Asia before the Mongol invasion of the 13th century. Today they number over 20 million, of which 1 million live in Tajikistan predominantly in the northern and western parts of the republic.

Tajik woman dressed in traditional ikat *(atlas) silk dress plays the drum at a Tajik festival.*

In addition, there are the Pamiris, also known as Badakhshanis, who reside in the Gorno-Badakhshan province. Like the Tajiks, the Pamiris are of Iranian descent and number in the tens-of-thousands.

Another group indigenous to Central Asia are the Bukharan Jews, who along with the European Jewry, numbered 14,000 in Tajikistan. In the fall of 1992, when the civil war in Tajikistan was full-blown, the Israeli government evacuated most of Tajikistan's Jewish population. It is thought that fewer than 2,000 Jews reside in Tajikistan in 2004. A number of Tajik Jews have immigrated and settled in Colorado.

There are also a number of non-indigenous ethnic groups that migrated to the region after Russia captured most of Central Asia in the 19th century. Still larger numbers of Russians, Belorussians, Georgians, Osetians, Armenians, Germans, and Koreans flooded the region after the Soviet take-over in the last century.

What People Say about the Tajiks

People who know Tajiks attest to the indefatigable Tajik spirit. According to Coloradan **Jonathan Zartman:** *"Tajik cultural nationalists claim that their highest cultural values are hospitality, openness, and serving the stranger. In other words, these are the values of which most Tajiks really are proud. This can be seen in the small figurines for sale in the art salon gallery across from the presidential palace in Dushanbe. One is a squatting old man holding a cup of tea in one had and 'nan' (bread) in the other… Tajiks say this symbolizes that a Tajik will share his last piece of bread with anyone who will sit and drink tea."*

Photo courtesy of Nazir Sharipov

The delightful clothes of the men and women from the villages (qishloqs) *are another interesting feature. Men wear the traditional* joma *(a knee-long jacket) tied at the waist with a colorful* mionband *(kerchief). Their* toqii *(skullcap), with its paisley design, distinguishes the wearers by region. Women wear a* kurta, *made of soft, colorful, bright silk, and a* shalvor *(long pants) with decorative cuffs* (sheroza).

Boulder residents **Peter and Sophia Stoller** have hosted over a dozen Tajik students: *"It's a wonderful way to learn about Dushanbe and to make friends….We have appreciated all that our students have shared with us and all that we have learned. We value their friendships. The Tajik students have been the tops."*

Ron and Marlies West were in Dushanbe 1999 in with a group from Boulder: *"We were tremendously impressed with the hospitality of the Tajik people, the sincerity of the hand-over-heart greeting, and the colorful beauty of the dress of the Tajik women. We were so moved that we became very active in the affairs of the BDSC."*

Miriam Allen: *"Fifteen years ago a wonderful young boy from Dushanbe came into our life and home through a student exchange. We were instantly and forever bonded. He is a cherished member of our family. If you concentrate on what we have in common with others, differences vanish. Sensitivity and appreciation of different cultures are the result. People-to-people exchanges are the country's greatest foreign policy assets."*

Tajik Stars

Muhammad Asimov (Osimi), Philosopher and Educator
Muhammad Asimov (Osimi) was born in Khujand on August 25, 1920, to peasant parents. After graduating from Samarkand State University in 1941, he served in the Soviet Army from 1941–1946 as a commander of an artillery battery near Leningrad and was badly wounded. From 1946–1952, he was a head teacher and Director of the Department of Physics of the Leninabad (Khujand) State Pedagogical Institute. From 1952–1955, he was a post-graduate student of sociology at the Academy of Social Sciences of the Soviet Union. From 1956–1962, he was the Associate Minister of Education. In 1965, he became the President of the Academy of Sciences of Tajikistan. He received his doctorate in philosophy in 1971, the same year he became a professor. He was the Chairman of "Paivand," the "Tajik Society of Cultural Relations with Compatriots Abroad". His main areas of research were philosophy and the history of science and culture of the Tajiks and of the nations of the East. Asimov is one of the founders and the main scientific editor of the *Tajik Encyclopedia*. He was honored with the Jawaharlal Nehru award in 1983 for his promotion of the scientific and cultural relations between Central Asia and India. He also worked for UNESCO and wrote *The History of Civilization of Central Asia.*

Mu'min Qano'atov, Poet

Mu'min Qano'atov was born on May 20, 1923, in the Autonomous Badakhshan region of the Pamirs into a family of farmers. He graduated from Tajikistan State University in 1956, where he studied philology and history. From 1961–1966, he was the chief editor of the poetry section of the "Voice of the Orient." The tone of Qanoatov's poetic career was set by his first collection entitled "The Flame" (1960). He is a master in finding representative characters from the working class to precisely communicate his thoughts. To tell the story of Anna, for instance, he spent a few months among the workers at the Norak hydro-electric dam, getting to know the work and life there. In "Story of the Fire," he tells us about how Anna's hopes for reunion with her husband were dashed daily. Innovation, precision, and realism are the hallmarks of Qano'atov's poetry. At present, he lives in Bishkek, Kyrgyzstan where he moved with his family in the late 1990s.

Sayf Rahimov, Cinematographer and Author

Sayf Rahimov was born into a farming family in the village of Dektur near Kulab on November 20, 1953. He graduated from Tajikistan State University with a degree in Persian Language and Literature in 1975. Soon after, he became an Assistant Cinematographer at Tajik Television. In 1999, he became the Minister of Radio and Television of Tajikistan, revamping state programming and introducing a number of programming initiatives with lasting influence on Tajik broadcasting. Rahimov has a unique style of writing. His stories delve deeply into the realities of life and, with a philosopher's eye, identify recurring problems. His study of the youth culture of Tajikistan is particularly of great importance. Rahimov's first story entitled "Sitorahoi Sari Tanur" ("Stars Over the Oven Pit") was first published in 1982. By the time his "Az Yodho, Az Yodho..." ("Memories, O Memories") was published in 1988, he was recognized as a trend-setter for Tajik prose. Many of Rahimov's poems have been published in Moscow and translated into different languages of the Republics of the Former Soviet Union. Rahimov's award-winning feature film entitled Sitorahoi Sari Tanur was based on his psychological probing originally set forth in his novella of the same name. He was assassinated in Dushanbe in 2000.

Muhammadjon Shukurov, Research Scholar & Literary Critic

Muhammadjon Shukurov was born in Bukhara on October 30, 1926. He graduated from the Department of Tajiki Language and Literature of the Dushanbe Pedagogical Institute in 1945. He joined the staff of the Rudaki Institute of Languages and Literatures as a Scientific Worker. In 1955, Shukurov received his doctorate degree at the Institute of Oriental Studies of the Academy of Sciences of the Soviet Union. In 1957, he became the Head of the Division of Contemporary Tajik Literature. In 1987, he became a full member of the Academy of Sciences of Tajikistan. Shukurov is an untiring contributor to the promotion of the Iranian culture of the Tajiks. He has researched and presented many of the biographies of the prominent figures of Tajikistan. His contributions include Paivandi Zamonho va Paivandi Khalqho (Temporal Connections and Connections Among People, 1982); Zaboni Mo, Hastii Mo (Our Language, Our Existence, 1991); and Khuroson Ast Injo (This is Khurasan, 1996). In 1944, he won the Rudaki State Prize, as well as awards for Friendship Among People (1986), the Red Banner of Courage, the 100th Anniversary of the Birth of Lenin Prize, and the Dusti Prize (1999). In 1991, Shukurov was recognized as a Distinguished Contributor to Science in Tajikistan.

Akbar Tursunov, Scientist and Philosopher

Akbar Tursunov was born into a family of workers near Khujand on October 1, 1939. He graduated from Tajikistan State University with a degree in physics and mathematics in 1961. He received his doctorate degree in philosophy in 1982 from the Institute of Philosophy of the Academy of Sciences of the Soviet Union. From 1986-1992, he was the Director of the Institute of Oriental Studies of the Academy of Sciences of Tajikistan. In 1993, he was elected the President of the National Association of Political Scientists of Tajikistan, an association

that he established. Tursunov has produced an extensive amount of literature on philosophy, literature, history of science, and on the history and culture of the Tajiks. Tursunov left Tajikistan in 1994, and since 1996 has been a Visiting Curator for Central Asian Ethnology at the University of Pennsylvania.

Malika Sabirova, Ballerina

Malika Sabirova was a Tajik actor and ballerina. She was born into a family of Dushanbe musicians on May 33, 1942. She attended the Leningrad Choreography Academy. And was a solo artist of the Aini Theater for Opera and Ballet. She was one of the outstanding representatives of the Russian school of classical dance. Her characters were complete and multi-dimensional. They included the loyal and hurt Odette, cunning and ravishing Odila, and the coquettish and carefree Liza. She became a People's Artist of the Soviet Union in 1947 and won many other honors. Sabirova died in 1982.

Djamshed Usmonov, Film-maker

Djamshed Usmonov was born in Asht, Tajikistan, on January 13, 1965. He graduated Dushanbe Fine Arts School, Theatre Section, and has been working in the movie industry since 1986 as a director, producer, and editor. He has written scripts for fiction films, animation and documentary films. His 2001 film "The Angel on the Right Shoulder', which he wrote and directed, has won world-wide acclaim. Usmonov set Angel on the Right in his own hometown, and cast his own mother and brother in the lead roles. The film was selected for Un Certain Regard at the 2002 Cannes Film Festival. He has also directed "The Well" (2000), "The Flight of the Bee" (1998), and "The Man" (1997). He has lived in Moscow since 1993.

About Boulder, Colorado

Half way around the world from Dushanbe, Boulder sits on the banks of Boulder Creek in the Boulder Valley, 5430 feet above sea level. Boulder grew slowly after first being organized in 1859 as a supply base for miners seeking their fortunes in gold and silver in the nearby mountains. The University of Colorado was founded in Boulder City in 1874. Now more than 26,000 students study at CU, 4% of whom are international students. Boulder encompasses about 22.5 square miles at the foot of the Rocky Mountains and has a population of 94,763. The community is known for its recreational opportunities and beautiful natural surroundings, including open space acquired over the past 20 years. It is also known as a leading city for growth control as urban sprawl becomes a contentious issue statewide.

Photo courtesy of Boulder Conventions and Visitors Bureau

Boulder's summer Farmers Market convenes every Wednesday and Saturday right in front of the Boulder-Dushanbe Teahouse.

An Interview with Iraj Bashiri about Tajiks and Tajikistan

Professor Iraj Bashiri is a professor of Central Asian Studies at the University of Minnesota. He has an MA in Linguistics (1968) and a PhD in Iranian Linguistics (1972), both from the University of Michigan. A distinguished College of Liberal Arts teacher (1980), he has an honorary doctorate degree in history and culture from Tajikistan State University in the Name of Lenin (1996), and is an honorary International member of the Academy of Sciences of Tajikistan (1997).

Dr. Bashiri has traveled extensively in Iran and Central Asia. Recently, he edited the online and printed texts of "Tajikistan in the 20th Century," for Radio Free Europe/Radio Liberty. His "Prominent Tajik Figures of the Twentieth Century" provides a comprehensive account of the lives of some 600 scholars, literary figures, politicians, and other professionals who have contributed to the promotion of Tajik culture.

Question: What would Tajiks like Americans to know most about Tajikistan and Tajik culture?

Iraj Bashiri: Tajiks would like Americans to know that Tajikistan has a long and glorious history with a rich tradition of guest-host relationship. Historically, Tajiks relate themselves to the House of Saman (875-999), but ancient history recalls their legendary and historical personages to include Kaykhusrau, the legendary king who announced the coming of the Prophet Zoroaster; Cyrus the Great, who founded the first world empire; and Abu al-Qasim Firdowsi, who revived the Persian language and immortalized Iranian culture. Most of all, however, Tajiks would like Americans to take note of the artistic, literary, and scientific contributions of their ancestors to world civilization.

Question: If the Boulder-Dushanbe Teahouse gift conveys a message from the Tajik people to Americans, what do you think that message is?

Iraj Bashiri: I believe the Boulder-Dushanbe Teahouse gift conveys a message of international cooperation. The teahouse is centered on the theme of Hakim Jamal al-Din Ilyas Nizami's *Haft Paikar* ("The Seven Beauties") (editor's note: this is the theme of the water sculpture in the Teahouse), one of the earliest works in Perso-Tajik literature wherein a young prince learns about the existence of beauties outside his realm. He brings those beauties to his realm and creates for each a pavilion that duplicates her cherished traditions. In that sense, the Teahouse is a Tajik seed deposited in the Boulder ground. The Tajiks' hope is that in time this seed will foster cultural understanding and cooperation beneficial to both cultures.

For the past five years, I have watched the interaction between the Boulderites and the citizens of Dushanbe. I have also observed the care with which the people of Boulder have responded to the needs of the people of Dushanbe, especially during the Tajik Civil War when the Tajiks were in dire need of food and medicine. The seed has begun to sprout and the cultural understanding and cooperation that the Tajiks had hoped for are being realized.

Question: What is your opinion about Boulder's gift concept, a Cyber Café learning center, for Dushanbe?
Iraj Bashiri: I think it is a forward-looking concept. Originally, I thought a courthouse, representing democracy and rule of law, to be built in Dushanbe by masons from Boulder, would be an appropriate gift. Given the Tajiks' penchant for knowledge, a Cyber Café will serve a similar purpose. The list of Tajik personalities who have contributed to the great western civilization that we enjoy today is immense. Avicenna, Al-Biruni, Razi, Rumi, and Firdowsi are only the most cited. They examined the thoughts of the ancient Greeks, revised and enhanced that ancient legacy and turned it over to posterity for application. What enabled these thinkers of the 11th and 12th centuries to make such immense contributions was a number of Nizamiyyahs instituted by the caliphs in Baghdad and other major cities to promote scientific work. These institutes placed at the disposal of the scholars all the tools necessary to carry out their research. The Cyber Café will be a modern Nizamiyyah for preparing tomorrow's Avicennas and al-Birunis.

PART 3

The Meaning of the Boulder– Dushanbe Teahouse

Ta'rikh

The History of the Boulder–Dushanbe Teahouse

"The Sister Cites program is an important resource to the negotiations of governments in letting the people themselves give expression to their common desire for friendship, goodwill, and cooperation for a better world for all."

—PRESIDENT DWIGHT D. EISENHOWER

The Boulder-Dushanbe Teahouse was born out of a grassroots sister city effort by the citizens of Boulder, first called the Soviet Sister City Project (SSCP) and later Boulder-Dushanbe Sister Cities (BDSC). Its history can be divided into three waves:

- The Soviet Sister City Project (1982-1987), which led to the pairing with Dushanbe;
- Boulder-Dushanbe Sister Cities' effort to assemble and open the Teahouse (1988-1998); and
- The effort to provide Dushanbe with a reciprocal gift (1998-present).

Master Tajik woodcarvers Manon Khaidarov and Mirpulat Mirakhmatov, who came to Boulder to supervise the assembly of the Choihona, take a tea break from their work.

The First Wave: *The Soviet Sister City Project (1982-1987)*

The first chapter in the history of the Boulder-Dushanbe Teahouse began in 1982 when a group of political activists in Boulder brought together by Mary Hey and Sophia Stoller decided to do something positive at the grass-roots level to improve the frosty relations between the USSR and the US. Their aim was "to get to know people very

unlike ourselves and, through understanding, to make the world just a little bit better…
and to have some fun on the road to understanding."[46] Just as the "Founding Fathers"
set forth the principles and values for young America, this group successfully built an
organization and mobilized people in Boulder intent on bringing about change in the
world through "citizen diplomacy" at a time when America and the USSR were still in
the midst of the Cold War.

"This was a time in our history when the Soviet Union was characterized by our
government and much of the media as the 'evil empire'," Mary Axe said. In the pre-
ceding four years, President Carter had recommended that NATO modernize and
increase the alliance's military forces, signaling the end of détente. He called for a
major military build-up and imposed sanctions against the USSR in reaction to its
invasion of Afghanistan, including a grain embargo, decreased scientific and cultural
exchanges; a boycott of the 1980 Moscow Olympic Games, and failure to ratify SALT
II; and he had signed a Presidential Directive calling for the capacity to wage limited
and protracted nuclear war.

Over 800,000 protesters marched in New York against nuclear arms on June 12, 1982,
nine months before newly-elected President Reagan proposed the Strategic Defense
Initiative, popularly known as Star Wars. Later that year Congress authorized MX
missile procurement and development. Korean Air Flight 007 was shot down by a
Soviet jet fighter in Soviet airspace, killing all 269 aboard. And the United States
began deployment of INF missiles (Pershing II) in West Germany.

Mary Hey, co-founder of the Soviet Sister City project, reflected on the events of
those days:

> *"It was the winter of 1982, and the Cold War was raging. Sophia Stoller and I*
> *were introduced in a church basement, and struck up a conversation about the*
> *frightening prospect of war with the Soviet Union. We both actively opposed the*
> *arms race, but wasn't there something positive we could do? We found ourselves*

amazed at how little we actually knew about the United States' mortal enemy, and wondered if perhaps others would also like to know more. We wondered how we could ever manage to meet a real live Soviet citizen."[47]

The steering committee of the SSCP decided on a two-prong strategy: to learn more about the Soviet Union and to actively look for a sister city there. Hundreds of sympathetic Boulder citizens attended a series of events and programs over several years to educate themselves and promote a rational understanding between the peoples of the US and USSR. These included lectures on history, language, politics, and science, several Russian Spring Festivals, musical and cultural events, and a multiyear Soviet Film Festival. SSCP's mailing list had grown to over 700 people.

Regarding the sister-city search, Mary Hey continues:

"We were actively pursuing a [sister city] relationship. I visited the Soviet Embassy in Washington, D.C., several times, we wrote repeated letters to faceless bureaucrats, and finally, having been studiously ignored, simply chose Dushanbe as our city and pursued officials there directly."[48]

Volume I Number 1 of the Soviet Sister City Project Newsletter dated October, 1985.

The principal reason that it took so long to establish a sister city with the Soviet Union was that the Soviets had a criterion that their foreign sister cities must have a population of 100,000, and Boulder's population in the mid-1980s was 80,000. A key event was when Mary Hey presented a Russian diplomat at the Soviet Embassy in D.C. with a folder of newspaper clippings and flyers about their monthly programs. When he saw a photo of a Boulder *balalaika* band, his mood changed.

Within weeks of that moment SSCP heard that the Soviets had revised their policy to state that foreign cities should have a population of 100,000 *or possibly 80,000.*

In fact, Dushanbe was chosen after several thwarted attempts to find a suitable match. The first lead to Dushanbe came through University of Colorado physicist James Scott, who had worked there for many months. He persuaded the SSCP that Dushanbe was the best choice for Boulder and attempted to deliver its first letter to Dushanbe's mayor. He was unsuccessful because, he was told, the mayor was away on "official business." Joe Allen, director of World Data Center-A for Solar-Terrestrial Physics at the National Oceanic and Atmospheric Administration (NOAA) in Boulder was the next to visit. He planned to attend a scientific symposium in Dushanbe in August of 1985. Members of the SSCP asked him if he would hand-deliver a letter from Boulder Mayor Ruth Correll to Dushanbe Mayor Nabi Shorakhmanov encouraging Dushanbe to become Boulder's sister city. Joe recalled this about that groundbreaking trip:

> "…after some hesitation, friends of mine from Moscow set up the situation in which I met with the mayor of Dushanbe and the head of the Tajik Academy of Sciences… I asked [Soviet scientist] friends from Moscow… whether they could assist me in carrying out the delegated assignment [of delivering a proposal to set up a sister city relationship to the mayor]. They first questioned why Boulder would want to have as its Sister City some obscure place such as Dushanbe, when it [Boulder] was so prominent a "Science City" that it could have chosen any place in the Soviet Union. However, they agreed to help, and invoked their positions in the USSR Academy of Sciences to more-or-less force the issue in Dushanbe. The mayor and President of the Tajik Academy were strongly encouraged to host a meeting with me and to accept the honor being offered."[49]

Mayor Shorakhmanov reportedly said at that meeting, "You people in Boulder are very persistent!" The SSCP finally knew that it was having some effect.

Meanwhile, relations with the Soviet Union were slowly warming up. At the November 21, 1985 Geneva Summit Presidents Reagan and Gorbachev issued a joint statement on cooperation in arms reductions with a goal of 50 percent reductions of nuclear arms. On January 15, 1986, Gorbachev proposed eliminating *all* nuclear weapons over the next 15 years, contingent on United States backing off SDI. Reagan applauded the proposal, but would not change position on SDI and supported a principle of 50 percent reduction as agreed to in 1985. At the December 1987 Washington Summit Meeting, Reagan and Gorbachev signed a treaty eliminating INF weapons and agreed to work toward completing the START (Strategic Arms Reduction Talks) agreement.

> *"Your efforts to open channels of communication between the citizens of the Soviet Union and the citizens of the United States are vital steps in the long march toward world peace. It is the foundation of mutual understanding that a long lasting peace will eventually rest."*
> —Letter from Colorado Governor Richard Lamm to the Soviet Sister City Project, July 23, 1984

Photo courtesy of Mary Hey

Breakthrough: Mary Hey meets with Dushanbe Mayor Nabi Shorakhmanov in October 1986. Also on that trip were Boulderites Tom and Jo Spencer, and Cheryl and Sam Sussman.

In April 1986, an executive vice-president of Sister Cities International traveled to Moscow to discuss setting up ten Sister Cities pairings with American cities, including Boulder. Six months later, Mary Hey was warmly received in Dushanbe by government officials. She delivered letters from Mayor Ruth Correll and the Boulder Chamber of Commerce, gifts and samples of Boulder products, and children's art created especially for Dushanbe, and also suggested a visit to Boulder. In May 1987, after five years of struggle to link up with a Soviet city in order to promote peace, a delegation led by the new Mayor of Dushanbe, Maksud Ikramov, visited Boulder. The Soviet Sister City Project and the City of Boulder finally officially sealed their relationship with Dushanbe, creating only the ninth US-Soviet sister city tie. It was during that visit that Mayor Ikramov mentioned that his city wanted to present the people of Boulder a token of friendship: a traditional hand-crafted Tajik *choihona*.

Mayor Ikramov's gesture reflected the Tajik cultural values of generosity, gift-giving, and friendship. It coincided with the transformation of the Soviet Sister City Project, led by Mary Hey and Sophia Stoller, into Boulder-Dushanbe Sister Cities, initially led by Marcia Johnston, and opened the second chapter in the story of the Boulder-Dushanbe Teahouse.

The names of many of the people who were instrumental in creating the Boulder-Dushanbe Teahouse are inscribed in the Teahouse art. On the carved plaster panel on the west wall, are the names of the late Dushanbe Mayor Maksud Ikramov (left) and the Tajik architect Lado Shanidze among others. Both men died an early death and never saw the Boulder-Dushanbe Teahouse erected. Before becoming mayor in 1987, Ikromov had been an engineer. After serving five years as mayor, he was imprisoned during the Tajik Civil War. He was released from prison in March 1993 and served a second short term as mayor. Maksud Ikramov was killed in an automobile accident near Samarkand on December 23, 1997, six months before the opening of the Boulder-Dushanbe Teahouse.[50]

Boulder-Dushanbe Sister Cities (BDSC)

BDSC has continued the Soviet Sister City Project mission of fostering of friendship and mutual understanding between the citizens of Boulder and Dushanbe. BDSC has a growing and dedicated membership that continues to this day to contribute time, money, and expertise to BDSC's many projects, just as the hundreds of volunteers had supported the SSCP through the "first wave" of establishing the organization and securing a Soviet sister city.

The mission of Sister Cites International (SCI) (**www.sister-cities.org**) is to "promote peace through mutual respect, understanding, and cooperation—one individual, one community at a time." Sister city affiliations between the United States and other nations began shortly after World War II and developed into a national initiative when President Dwight D. Eisenhower proposed the "People-to-People" program at a White House conference in 1956. President Eisenhower's intention was to involve individuals and organized groups at all levels of society in citizen diplomacy, with the hope that personal relationships, fostered through sister city, county, and state affiliations, would lessen the chance of future world conflicts. SCI represents over 2,100 communities in 122 countries around the world.

Since 1987, BDSC activities have included: sponsorship of cultural exchanges, tours to Tajikistan, sponsorship of student exchanges, promotion of "sister school" relationships, facilitating the sharing of medical knowledge through physician exchanges and medical training, providing computers and clothing to Tajik schools, non-profits, and orphanages, shipping humanitarian aid in response to the devastating civil war in the early 1990s, fostering an exchange of knowledge about environmental conservancy, sponsorship of local educational programs about Tajik culture, participation in local international fairs and festivals, publishing a newsletter covering BDSC activities and Tajik news, and supporting individual efforts to build friendship and good-will with the people of Tajikistan.

A Boulder-Dushanbe Teahouse Chronology

October 1983 The Soviet Sister City Project (SSCP) is founded.

January 1984 Boulder City Council votes unanimously to support efforts to establish a sister city in the Soviet Union.

August 1985 While attending a symposium in Dushanbe, Boulder scientist Joe Allen hand-delivers a letter proposing a Sister City relationship to Dushanbe Mayor Nabi Shorakhmanov.

April 1986 The first American/Soviet Sister Cities Conference takes place in Ward, Colorado, attracting 75 participants from 24 US cities. Also, an executive vice-president of Sister Cities International travels to Moscow to discuss setting up ten Sister Cities pairings, including Boulder.

October 1986 Five Boulder "citizen diplomats" led by SSCP President Mary Hey visit Dushanbe and are welcomed by Mayor Shorakhmanov, who agrees in principle to a Sister Cities relationship.

May 1987 Dushanbe Mayor Maksud Ikramov visits Boulder to sign the Sister Cities agreement and mentions that Dushanbe will present the people of Boulder with a traditional Tajik Teahouse. Also, a 32-member tour group from Boulder visits Dushanbe.

Fall 1987 The SSCP becomes the Boulder-Dushanbe Sister Cities (BDSC), now led by new President Marcia Johnston, who forms a committee to begin planning for receiving and building the Teahouse.

Fall 1988 Boulder Mayor Jourgensen appoints a Teahouse Taskforce of citizens to consider whether to accept the gift of the *Choihona*.

May 1989 On Taskforce's recommendation, City Council votes to accept the gift of the *Choihona*.

June 1989 The Teahouse Trust is formed to plan shipping, fundraising, publicity, and related matters.

August 1990 BDSC raises $35,000 to pay for shipping costs and the *Choihona* arrives in Boulder, packed in over 200 shipping crates. It is stored at a city-owned facility.

September 11, 1990 Mayors Durgin and Ikramov sign a protocol calling for a reciprocal gift of a "Boulder Restaurant," and cultural, educational, scientific, technology, and sports exchanges.

April 1991 City Council unanimously accepts the Citizens Committee recommendation to build the Teahouse on 13th Street.

April 1993 City Council votes 7-0 with 2 abstentions to locate the *Choihona* on 13th Street just north of the Boulder Art Center, as originally recommended by the Civic Center Task Force.

October 1993 Dedication ceremonies at the *Choihona* during BDSC's 10th anniversary celebration, with Zubaidullo Zubaidov, head of Protocol for Tajikistan, as honored guest.

September 1994 The Teahouse Trust signs a 20-year lease with the City of Boulder for the Teahouse.

May 1995 National Endowment for the Arts awards $25,000 to the Teahouse project.

Summer 1995 Pete Jensen of Chrisman, Bynum & Johnson draws up sublease between operator and Trust; work done *pro bono*.

Spring 1996 Teahouse Trust arranges $1 million bank loan with a consortium of six Boulder banks for Teahouse construction.

Fall 1996 It was disclosed that the City had been notified by the EPA that the site of the Teahouse was designated as a potential Superfund clean-up site as a coal gasification plant had once been located on the site. The banks withdrew their loan agreement. City Manager Tim Honey proposed borrowing from city funds to cover Teahouse construction.

March 1997 Boulder City Council votes approval of an ordinance to fund construction of the Teahouse, 5 yes, 3 no, 1 abstention.

July 1997 Sara and Lenny Martinelli sign lease to operate Teahouse restaurant facility. Groundbreaking ceremonies are held.

September 1997 Construction of the Teahouse begins.

December 1997 Master woodcarvers Manon Khaidarov and Mirpulat Mirakhmatov along with Kodir Rakhimov, plaster carver and painter, arrive in Boulder to assist with Teahouse construction.

February 1998 Victor Zabolotnikov, ceramist, arrives from Dushanbe.

May 15, 1998 Dedication/opening ceremonies for Teahouse with the Honorable Rashid Alimov, Tajikistan Ambassador to the United Nations, and former Mayor Guggenburger of Klagenfurt, Austria (one of Dushanbe's sister cities) in attendance.

Summer 1998 A reciprocal gift committee forms to decide on an appropriate gift for Dushanbe.

March 20, 1999 First annual Tajik New Year (Navruz) is celebrated at Teahouse.

August 1999 Teahouse hosts fist annual educational Tea Festival.

Fall 1999 100,000th visitor enters Teahouse.

April 2000 First Children's Tea Party held in Teahouse.

July 2001 First Bar Mitzvah party held in Teahouse.

2001 Teahouse named "Top Tea" destination in Denver area by *5280 Magazine*.

2001–2004 BDSC holds series of fund-raiser dinners at Teahouse for Cyber café gift project.

Summer 2002 Tajik artisan Kodir Rakhimov makes repairs to Teahouse art.

2002 Teahouse named "Best Romantic Restaurant" in Denver area by *Westword.com*.

July 2003 Teahouse Proprietor Lenny Martinelli's lease is renewed by City for five more years.

September 2003 First wedding held in Teahouse.

2003 Teahouse named "Best Place to Eat" in Boulder by *Boulder Weekly*.

February 2004 First annual Youth Exchange and Study (YES) Islamic Leadership Summit reception held at the Teahouse with Congressman Mark Udall as honoured guest. Co-sponsored by Sister Cities International and AYUSA. BDSC Fashion Show held at Teahouse raises $2490. Organizers were Lee Bentz, Leslie Hindes, and Mary Barnett.

March 2004 5th Annual Tajik New Year (Navruz) Party celebrated at Teahouse.

The Second Wave: The Effort to Assemble and Open the Teahouse (1988-1998)

Once the reality of the gift settled in, Boulder Mayor Linda Jourgensen formed a citizens taskforce in June 1989 to advise her on the feasibility of accepting such a gift from Dushanbe. When future historians look back at Boulder at the close of the 20th century, they will certainly comment on the how the Boulder-Dushanbe Teahouse project held the attention of the city's residents and how it continuously sent ripples through City Council, the art community, and the local press. One couldn't walk into a barbershop, beauty salon, bar, or social event without hearing opinions about the *Choihona*, or, as it was often erroneously called, "the Russian Teahouse."

• Should it even be accepted?

• Should tax-payer's money be spent for its site and construction?

• What was in it for Boulder?

• If accepted, where should it be located?

Some people in Boulder made jokes, suggested unusual return gifts, made it a major campaign issue, or conjoined the gift with the evils of Communism, the Russian occupation of Afghanistan, the needs of homeless people in Boulder, tourism, Boulder's image, and taxes. It raised important questions, and it stirred controversy, yet most people were curious about it and couldn't wait to see it in person.

Boulder-Dushanbe Teahouse Fact Sheet

• The largest gift ever given by the people of the Soviet Union to the people of the United States

• The only Central Asian Teahouse in the Western Hemisphere

• The only other two known Central Asian teahouses outside of Central Asia are in Klagenfurt, Austria, which is another of Dushanbe's Sister Cities, and Berlin, Germany[7]

• Shipped in over 200 sea-going containers—total weight 30 tons

• Cost $800,000 to erect plus approximately $300,000 raised by the Teahouse Trust

• Valued at more than one million dollars

• 40 Tajik craftsmen worked on the project

• Interior area is 2343 square feet

• Dimensions: 20' tall; 44' deep; 55' wide

After much debate and significant efforts of the Teahouse Trust, the City of Boulder decided to accept the gift. On September 11, 1990, Boulder Mayor Leslie Durgin and

Dushanbe Mayor Maksud Ikramov signed a protocol that said: "Subsequent to the installation of the teahouse, BDSC will exercise its best efforts to raise sufficient funds to construct a 'Boulder Restaurant' or other mutually agreed-upon structure in Dushanbe, including necessary furniture and technical equipment."[6] It also called for a wide range of cultural, educational, and scientific exchanges and cooperation.

> "The Teahouse is like a flower. We hope it brings people happiness and enjoyment. People will come, drink coffee or tea, and look up, and it will make their souls happy."
>
> —Mirpulat Mirakhmatov, master Tajik wood carver who worked on the Teahouse project

An extraordinary letter to the editor of the *Boulder Camera* on October 23, 1988 is a high water mark of the feelings of people in Boulder at the time. (It's notable that eighteen out of its twenty sentences end in either an exclamation mark or a question mark.)

> *Editor:*
>
> *What a wonderful good fortune for Boulder to be given a Tadjikan (sic) teahouse by Russia! Just in time! A new controversy! We were all getting bored with arguing where to put the library. Now we can argue over where to put the new teahouse.*
>
> *Should we put it downtown? Crossroads parking lot? The Watts-Hardy site? The greenbelt? Should we even accept it? Should we even accept it at all considering Afghanistan? Should we float a bond to pay for the land? Raise the sales tax? Should there be bicycle routes going to it? Can senior citizens walk to it?*
>
> *Will the lights at night disturb the neighbors? Should we close all the roads around it? Should it be made a nuclear-free zone? And how will we keep the deer from eating it? Oh, are we going to have fun!"*

Raising the Teahouse

Work on the traditional Teahouse art began in 1987 in Dushanbe and Khujand, a 2,000 year old city in the north of Tajikistan known for its arts and crafts. In Boulder, a corps of volunteers joined Mary Axe (President of Boulder-Dushanbe Sister Cities) and Vern Seieroe, a Boulder architect who volunteered to adjust the original drawings submitted by the Teahouse architect, the late Lado Shanidze, in order to conform to local standards and site. With other volunteers including Greg Lamberson, Bart Balis, Mohammad Aslamy, Jeffrey Moulton, and Brad Friedman, they began the heroic task of raising funds for construction, building community support, and planning for the long-awaited opening.

The art was shipped to Dushanbe in over 200 sea-going containers in 2343 pieces, a total weight of 30 tons. The shipment arrived in Boulder in August 1990. It was stored at a city-owned facility.

More than eight years passed before the Teahouse art was finally erected. City Council decided that the funds would come from a loan from the City Water Fund for $700,000 to cover construction costs, and that the location would be across from Central Park at 1770 13th Street, just two blocks south of Boulder's popular Pearl Street Mall. Lenny and Sara Martinelli, managers of Boulder's Naropa University's food services, Huckleberry Foods, won the contract to run the facility. Finally in September 1997 construction of the Teahouse began. It opened it doors to the public in May 1998.

The Teahouse has become the venue for several cultural and social events, including an annual tea symposium during the summer at which artists, tea experts, tea importers, estate owners, and blenders make presentations. It also has hosted an annual Tajik-Persian New Year (*Navruz*) celebration; the BDSC's annual meeting and numerous fund-raisers; and countless birthday parties, bar mitzvahs, and even weddings. More than 100,000 people visit the Teahouse annually. Since its opening, the Teahouse has truly become a gathering place for Boulder citizens in the traditional Tajik sense.

Mary Axe Looks Back on the Project

Mary Axe was President of Boulder-Dushanbe Sister Cities from 1987 to 1998. In this interview she looks back at the both the high and low points.

Question: How did you initially become interested in the BDSC project?

Mary Axe: Some 21 years ago, I was a co-founder of the Soviet Sister City Project (SSCP). I was deeply concerned about the threat of nuclear war. As someone who for many years had taken an active role in the peace movement, in 1982, I traveled to the Soviet Union to discover first-hand as much as I could about the people and culture of that nation.

Question: How did it come about that Dushanbe was chosen as our sister city?

Mary Axe: One our first tasks was trying to find a city in the then-USSR with whom to develop a sister city relationship. A local physicist, Jim Scott, had made several visits there and pointed out a number of similarities: Boulder and Dushanbe are located at about the same latitude, are close to high mountains, are home to several scientific research institutes and universities, and share similar climates.

Question: Looking back, what was/were the high point(s) and low point(s) of the 11 years?

Mary Axe: The high points were:
- Receiving $25,000 grant from the National Endowment for the Arts
- Casual meetings with hundreds of people over the years who expressed their support
- Seeing the groundswell of community support once construction actually began
- Witnessing the incredible skill and dedication of the Tajik and Boulder construction team

The low points were:
- Learning that the land on 13th St. intended for the Teahouse was a potential EPA superfund clean-up site, leading to the banks' withdrawal of a $1 million construction loan arranged by the Teahouse Trust
- Seeing letters to the editor and editorials in the newspapers calling the Teahouse a "white elephant"
- Learning of the deaths in late 1997 of both the architect of the Teahouse, Lado Shanidze, and Mayor Ikramov, and realizing they would never see the realization of their hard work and dreams

Question: What is so special about theTeahouse?

Mary Axe: It is an expression of the 2,700 year old Tajik culture, manifested both in the architecture and exquisite artistry, as well as in the boundless generosity of their spirit. Also, in 1987 when the gift was presented to us by Mayor Ikramov, the era of glasnost (openness) was in full swing in the Soviet Union. Expressions of long-repressed cultures were reawakening among minority ethnic groups, especially in their artistic heritage. The Teahouse was a result of this new openness.

Mary Axe, President of Boulder-Dushanbe Sister Cities from 1987-1998, relaxes at the Teahouse.

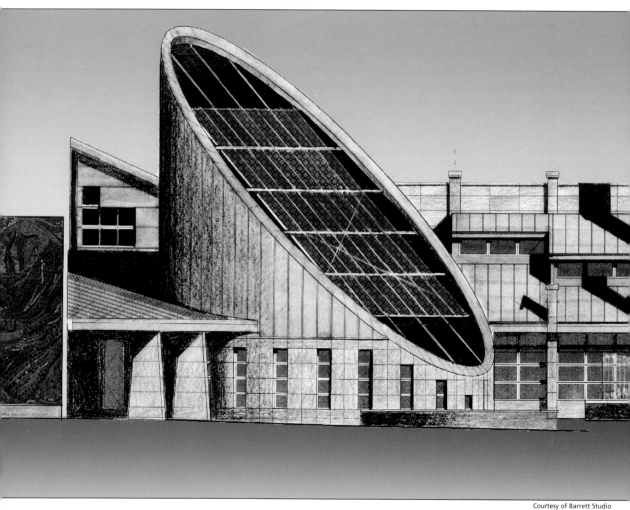

Courtesy of Barrett Studio

Dusti

The Reciprocal Gift: A Cyber Café for Dushanbe

"A millennium ago, this (Central Asian) region found its prosperity on the Silk Route; today the equivalent path may well be the Internet."

—U.S. SECRETARY OF STATE
MADELEINE ALBRIGHT, APRIL 18, 2000

The Third Wave: Reciprocating to Dushanbe *(1998-present)*

Ever since the Boulder-Dushanbe Teahouse opened for business in May 1998, people in Boulder have asked, "Now, what will we give them?"

The notion of a reciprocal gift for Dushanbe originated in May 1987 when Boulder Mayor Jourgensen and Dushanbe Mayor Ikramov agreed that once the Teahouse was erected, Boulder would reciprocate with a "Boulder restaurant" for Dushanbe. BDSC President Mary Axe stepped down in 1998 and was replaced by Jancy Campbell, who guided the organization through four years of preparations and fund-raising for the gift.

The proposed Cyber Café gift is meant to have a Boulder look. While BDSC continued to organize several projects and events that in one way or another related to its sister city, an enormous amount of energy and time was devoted to the planning and construction of the gift to Dushanbe that can be measured by eight "milestones."

MILESTONE 1: *The Formation of the BDSC Gift Committee*

Shortly after the Teahouse opened in May 1998, the idea of a Cyber Café-style restaurant as a gift emerged during brainstorming sessions by BDSC members and interested community members. The BDSC Reciprocal Gift Committee formed at this time and spent countless hours discussing what a "Boulder restaurant" meant, what the true needs of people and Dushanbe were, and how a gift that at least matched the quality and appeal of Dushanbe's gift could be financed. A consensus was reached that, like the Boulder Teahouse, the gift to Dushanbe needed to reflect the culture, life style, sensibilities and resources of Boulder and its people. The committee also felt that the "restaurant" suggested in the protocol should be much more than "just a place to eat dinner." That's when the idea of an Internet Café or "Cyber Café" emerged.

The "Reciprocal Gift Committee" organized itself into 12 sub-committees around tasks that needed to be accomplished. Many people from the community joined the committee at this point and regular meetings were held, usually in committee member David Barrett's architecture studio. The sub-committees' areas of focus were fund-raising, architecture, technology, education, construction, art, public relations, communication with Dushanbe, law, finances, transportation, and food services. The committee met once or twice a month from 1998 through 2004 to work toward realizing its collective dream of reciprocating for Dushanbe's extraordinary *Choihona* gift. Sophia Stoller was elected Chair of the Committee.

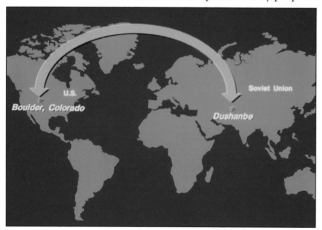

Reciprocating for a million-dollar gift from one of the most impoverished cities in the world to one of the wealthiest, as measured by per capita income, has been a daunting task for the BDSC Reciprocal Gift Committee, which has primarily relied on private donations.

The Benefits of a Cyber Café to Tajiks

Just as the Teahouse embodies Tajik craftsmanship, social customs, and aesthetic values, the Gift Committee felt that a Cyber Café should reflect Boulder's educational, human resources, technological, artistic, culinary and environmental profile.

The benefits of a Cyber Café to Tajiks could be considerable. For example, the vast majority of Tajiks do not have access to the Web at home or at work. As of 2003, Tajikistan was thought to have fewer than 5,000 Internet users. In addition, very few Tajiks own personal computers; instead they rely on a growing number of Internet cafes to access the Web. The notion of helping connect people in Dushanbe to the Internet was timely. Tajikistan is an isolated, poverty-stricken, land-locked country still recovering from the collapse of the Soviet Union and a civil war in the mid 90's. Although it has a very high literacy rate, it lacks technology, and, in particular, Internet connections.

The Internet, satellite-based cellular phone systems, and other global communications networks are becoming a potent catalyst for change in developing countries like Tajikistan. Not only do they facilitate widespread participation in social and political decision making, which is the nervous system of our global civilization, but they also enable a great leap forward by bringing a host of services and information directly to individuals and communities.

The committee members felt that a Cyber Café would allow citizens of Boulder's sister city to gain immediate access to educational programs, medical consultations, business opportunities, and social outlets. This "window to the world" would help fulfill the nearly insatiable human demand for access to knowledge and expose thousands of individuals to wider horizons. And new horizons would help shift perspectives to a more modern social and political outlook within a single generation. Furthermore, this gift would provide a seed for development of infrastructure and investment by other organizations, businesses, and governments. In developing nations, where such aid is provided, the success of the people in rising out of poverty and growing in economic empowerment is much greater than those that are just given simple relief aid with every new crisis.

Project architect Boulderite David Barrett, with input from a wide range of volunteer consultants and interested parties, suggested that the building should have an open, accessible design reflecting materials typical of Colorado, and it should include energy- and resource-saving features. The committee agreed and felt that the interior of the Cyber Café should reflect various Western U.S. themes. It should be a place where people can gather for food, drink, and conversation; have state-of-the-art computer workstations; display creative media by Boulder artists and craftspeople; and include a café area, a kitchen, a library of print, audio and video material, and space for other educational activities.

The BDSC Reciprocal Gift Committee felt strongly that a Cyber Café would be a valuable resource for the Tajiks who are in dire need of educational and communications technology.

The Benefits to Boulder

The gift committee felt strongly that people in Boulder would also benefit from this project in their communication with Tajiks through Cyber-space. They could connect to and learn with and from Tajiks in the context of the gift. A real-time video link could connect people in the *Choihona* with people in the Cyber Café. Students in the two cities could collaborate on learning projects.

The Protocol signed by the mayors of the two sister cities called for Boulder to send Dushanbe a "Boulder restaurant."

Courtesy of Barrett Studio

On November 19, 2003, CNN reported that an independent task force claimed America has a "serious deficit in global competence." The report also asserted that Americans are disconnected from the rest of the world at a time when anti-American sentiments run high over the war in Iraq and the aftermath of the September 11 terrorist attacks on New York and Washington. "September 11 was a warning that America's ignorance of the world is now a national liability." Former Education Secretary Richard Riley, honorary co-chairman of the Strategic Task Force on Education Abroad, said that "Our country cannot afford to remain ignorant of the rest of the world. The stakes are simply too high."[53]

World-renown cellist Yo-Yo Ma, who has facilitated cultural exchange with Central Asia through his Silk Road Project, sees the ancient Silk Road as the "Internet of Antiquity" and the World Wide Web as the "integral tool of contemporary cultural exchange."[3] "In the course of 25 years of performing in different parts of the world, I have become increasingly intrigued by the migration of ideas among communities," he said in the Silk Road Project Vision Statement.

MILESTONE 2: *The Mayor of Dushanbe Supports the Plan*

In January 2001, a delegation representing Boulder-Dushanbe Sister Cities was invited to visit Dushanbe. Delegation members were BDSC Gift Committee Chair and educator Sophia Stoller, technologists Ron Broome and Roger Kovacs, distance learning specialist George Peknik, and Project Architect David Barrett. They were warmly received by Dushanbe Mayor Makhmadsaid Ubaidulloev on Friday, January 26, in Tajikistan's House of Parliament, of which the mayor is also the Speaker. The mayor communicated his support for the project during a meeting, and the proposed Cyber Cafe was featured in a story on national television that evening.

> "We returned from Dushanbe feeling even more strongly that a Cyber Cafe is the right reciprocal gift for Dushanbe. Dushanbe's young people are eager to be connected to what's happening in the larger world."
> —Sophia Stoller, Chair, Reciprocal Gift Com.

After the meeting Mayor Ubaidulloev directed Dushanbe's Chief City Architect, Rustam Karimov, to reserve a piece of prime real estate for the cafe on the city's main cultural and educational thoroughfare, Rudaki Avenue. The site is located between Ferdowsi National Library and the Dushanbe Philharmonic Theater. The Gift Committee felt that the site was outstanding, as it is easily accessible to students and the general public in a truly beautiful part of the city. After the mayor designated the site, various members of the delegation took extensive photos and measurements of it. Project Architect David Barrett also had the opportunity to study the building site so he could begin work on the design of the building to take advantage of the site's geographical features.

Dushanbe Mayor Makhmadsaid Ubaidulloev exchanges gifts with BDSC Gift Committee Chair Sophia Stoller during the Gift Committee's visit to Dushanbe in January 2001.

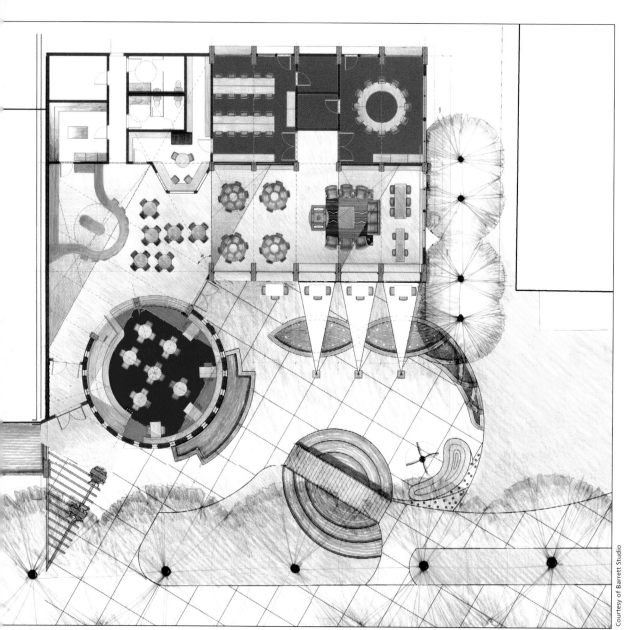

The Cyber Café will also have a library, lounge area, meeting rooms, kitchen, and a computing area.

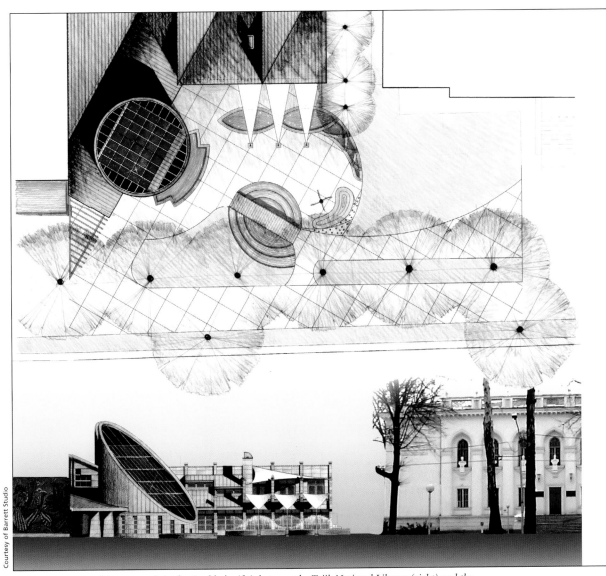

The proposed site for Boulder's gift is between the Tajik National Library (right) and the Philharmonic theater on Rudaki Avenue, which is nicknamed "Students Avenue". Six institutions of higher education are located on Rudaki Ave. or very near it, including Tajik State National University, Tajik State Pedagogical University, and Tajik Technical University.

The Architect's Thoughts on the Design of the Cyber Café

David Barrett is the Project Architect for the Cyber Café and a member of the Reciprocal Gift Committee. He visited Dushanbe in January 2001 to study the proposed building site, to meet with the Chief Architect for the city of Dushanbe, and to gather information to use in creating a design for the building.

Question: What was your thinking about the design of a Cyber Café for the people of Dushanbe?
David Barrett: Unlike Tajikistan, we in America don't have a deep-rooted history and architectural tradition from which to draw in the design of a building. The teahouse tells us who the Tajiks are, but designing a building that tells them who we are and what our values are is more complicated.

Question: Which of our values would you like to communicate in the Cyber-café?
David Barrett: Our Gift Committee, which is made up of people from all walks of life, identified several, including being open, having a free spirit, thinking in terms of possibilities and transformation—I like Bucky Fuller's concept of Americans being "verbs" as opposed to "nouns". Also we in the American West are inspired by nature.

Question: How are these values translated into the architecture of the café?
David Barrett: Our design team wanted to get away from closed-in box-shaped spaces so we have few interior walls. We opened up the interior to the outside, brought in lots of natural light, and connected the building to its natural surroundings.

Also, we felt that it would be a good idea to express our feelings about environmentalism and sustainable design principles. So we're going for solar voltaic cells to help power the computers, and provide for natural day lighting and ventilation. The building will also be accessible to all. We hope that like the teahouse it to be used by people of all ages.

Question: What building materials do you have in mind to use?
David Barrett: As much as possible, we plan to use materials that are available in Dushanbe, from concrete to the stones and boulders that are available there.

Question: Will there be any other Boulder or American West touches?
David Barrett: Yeah. We have a round kiva-like gathering place where performances and discussion could take place and where possibly the people of the two sister cities could link up using interactive video technology. And the outdoors playground and bridge will remind some people of what we have on Pearl Street. In the end, the most important thing is that the Tajiks will find the building beautiful in the same way that we feel about the teahouse, and that they won't get too tied up in analyzing the architecture itself. That's my goal.

The proposed Cyber Café would be a multi-use building with space for participating in educational activities, enjoying refreshments, using computers, and relaxing.

BDSC Events and Activities during this Period

Annually *Navruz* (Tajik-Persian New Year) was celebrated at the Teahouse each March and included Tajik food, Central Asian music and dancing, a crafts booth, and special activities for children, it has attracted an increasing number of citizens and their families, including many Tajiks. *Navruz* celebrates the first day of spring and is an ancient pre-Islamic holiday for Persians and Tajiks.

Annually BDSC maintained a booth at the annual Boulder Creek Festival and every Saturday throughout the spring and summer at the Boulder Farmers Market.

1999 A group of Tajik educators and editors visited Boulder. Among the visitors was the principal of School #20, Boulder Flatirons School's "sister school."

September 1999 A delegation of twelve from Boulder were invited to Dushanbe to attend the 1100th Anniversary of the Samonid State and the 8th Anniversary of Independence Day of the Republic of Tajikistan."

2000 Two Tajik exchange students arrive in Boulder. More than a dozen Tajiks have attended Boulder high schools as exchange students since then. Sergey Karimov and Maxime Harkovich. Teahouse named "Best Romantic Restaurant" in Denver area by *Westword.com.*

September 2000 BDSC hosted a reception at the Boulder Library after a showing of "The Silence," a film shot in Tajikistan and directed by celebrated Iranian filmmaker Mohsen Makhmalbaf.

October 2000 The BDSC Board hosted a potluck dinner for the visiting editors and educators from Tajikistan at the home of Joanne Karpinski.

2000–2001 In a tireless 2 year-long "PeaceRide 2000" fundraising effort, Boulderite and former Teahouse server Heath Wilson rode his bicycle from Boulder to Istanbul, Turkey, collecting donations in Boulder before

the trip and along the way. He rode for more than one year, camping along the way, and donated $18,000 to Dushanbe orphanages. BDSC provided support for that effort.

March 2002 Kodir Rakhimov, one of the Tajik artists who hand-crafted the Choihona, had a showing of fifteen of his oil paintings and plaster panels at the Boulder Museum of Contemporary Art.

June 2002 Long-time BDSC supporters Bob and Louise Dudley hosted a fund-raising musicale for the Cyber Café gift fund at their home. Victor Romasevich, a first violinist of the San Francisco Symphony, and Lena Lubotsky, pianist, performed a beautiful program of violin classics.

August 2002 Several BDSC members met in Aurora, Colorado, to honor the late Tajik scholar and humanist, Muhammad Osimi. The Osimi Cultural Center, which hosted the event, brings together the intellectuals of Tajikistan, Iran and Afghanistan and educates the new generation about their history and heritage. BDSC friends and members Dilorom and Mustafo Osimi hosted the event.

2003 The City of Dushanbe became an international city member of Sister Cities International due to the generosity of Boulderites Jean Dubofsky, Mr. and Mrs. Gary Meyers, and Mr. and Mrs. Kevin Kelly.

March 2003 Five Tajik visitors visited Boulder under the auspices of the State Department's International Visitor Program. They were in Boulder to learn more about disaster preparedness and response. Also, three other Tajiks visited Boulder to learn more about promoting tourism.

April 2003 Cynthia Butler and Ann and Andy Key shared a booth with the Silk Road Foundation during the Denver Botanic Gardens PlantAsia opening. Their efforts introduced the Cyber Café project and our mission to Denver-area plant lovers and raised funds through the sale of craft items.

May 2003 During the Memorial Day Weekend and the Boulder Creek Festival, BDSC hosted a series of activities associated with the fifth anniversary of the opening of the Teahouse and the design of a Cyber Cafe for Dushanbe, including a Cyber Cafe booth, a scale model of the Cyber Café, and a "cyber bridge" between Boulder and Dushanbe (with support from the Jared Polis Foundation). Also students and families at Flatirons Elementary School, Dushanbe's School #20 sister school, hosted a Talent Show to bring attention to Dushanbe and to help with fund-raising for the Cyber Café, and there was and a formal tea party with presentations by Mayor Toor and Tajik Ambassador to the US Hamrokhon Zaripov.

June 2003 BDSC sent 59 refurbished Pentium computers and clothing to Dushanbe. Eight Boulder and international organizations, including the Central Asian Development Agency (CADA) and Counterpart International teamed up with BDSC. The computers helped schools, orphanages, Non-Governmental Organizations (NGOs), and the Dushanbe City government connect to the Internet. Donors included the Jared Polis Foundation and AutoDesk. The Colorado Materials Exchange (COMEX) played an important "match-maker" role for securing the donations. Compassionate Stitchers, a local group, hand-knit several sweaters and other clothing included in the shipment.

June 2003 Barb Perin represented BDSC at the Sister City International (SCI) conference in St. Louis. SCI and other sister cities showed interested in the Dushanbe Cyber Café project.

July 23 BDSC Member Chair Mary Barnett and Membership Breakfast Chair Lemoine Dowd began holding "new member breakfasts." Their group, which called themselves "Friends of the Teahouse" got together to meet new friends and have fun supporting BDSC and the Cyber Café gift project.

July 2003 Holik Mirakhmatov, son of Mirpulat Mirakhmatov, one of the Tajik wood carvers of the Teahouse ceiling, visited Boulder. Mirpulat had passed away the previous year. He is remembered with warmth by all Boulderites who knew him. Holik saw his father's work for the first time during this visit.

2003–2004 The pen pal program between the Flatirons Elementary School and Dushanbe's School #1 continued, and the BDSC "Friends" Internet discussion board was launched. Fifty students from Dushanbe and 50 students from Chinook and Monarch High Schools discussed a variety of topics.

February 2004 BDSC, in collaboration with Sister Cities International, the Youth Exchange and Study program, and the Boulder Valley School District, took part in organizing the Youth Leadership Summit for more than 70 high school students from Muslim countries. Congressman Mark Udall hosted a reception at the Teahouse on February 27.

May 2004 The Central Asian Soccer Tour arrived in Boulder to give a presentation at the Teahouse and to play some exhibition games.

MILESTONE 3: *The Business Plan*

By the end of 2001, the committee had written a business plan and begun raising funds. Project Architect David Barrett had prepared schematic drawings of the modernistic building.

According to the BDSC Cyber Café Gift Business Plan:
- "The gift will be "a valuable symbol of friendship and understanding between our peoples and will greatly improve the ability of the people of Dushanbe to extend their awareness and communicate with the outside world.
- "The Cyber Café will be a showcase of state-of-the-art architecture and passive solar environmental control, daylighting, water-conserving technology, photovoltaic solar conversion to electricity, wavelength glazing, and high efficiency insulation.
- "The Cyber Café will reflect various Western themes including a circular 'kiva' room where people will gather for food, drink, and conversation, creative media by Boulder artists and craftspeople, a library of print, audio, and video material, and…computer workstations.
- "BDSC believes that we, as Americans, are stakeholders in building and maintaining friendship and stability in countries like Tajikistan that are vulnerable to political extremism and poverty. A bottom-up people-to-people initiative like this project is part of the solution to building and maintaining partnerships that connect isolated peoples with the rest of the world.
- "BDSC hopes that this project will serve as a model for other Non-Governmental Organizations…in resource-rich countries to assist their friends in the developing world cross the technological 'Digital Divide.'"

> *"Every time I open a newspaper, I am reminded that we live in a world where we can no longer afford not to know our neighbors."*
> —Yo-Yo Ma, Advocate of cultural exchange with Central Asian cultures

A Tajik's Perspective of the Reciprocal Gift Concept

Farida Asadova is a Tajik physician who lives in Dushanbe. Her daughter Adiba went to high school in Boulder and the studied at and graduated from DePauw University in Greencastle, Indiana.

"I think it was a great idea of Boulder people to give Dushanbe a Cyber Cafe as a reciprocal gift. As an ordinary resident of Dushanbe, I want to stress the need to develop ties between the people of the world and especially those Dushanbe City has Sister City links with. The collapse of the Soviet Union broke ties between the people and nations within the joint area we lived in. Now it is not easy even to send letters and get replies from our relatives living even in neighboring states, let alone the countries located far away.

"Your gift will provide us with an ample opportunity to be in touch with many people all over the world, and to learn a lot about the changes and developments taking place. Moreover, it will be a training center for those who would like to learn more about computers and English as well. And I think it will be the center of gatherings and communication for the young people.

"First of all, the younger generation will benefit from the activities of the Cyber Cafe. I am sure the intellectuals will get a lot from it as well as it will provide them with all kinds of information. The Internet fans will benefit from the cafe most of all. And one more point, if it will be able to provide its services to the population in their home PCs, which will be great.

"I want to tell you that my son and daughter learned a lot during being in US. They started to be more independent, practical, open and precise. They learned to rely on themselves. In this attitude our tradition is different. But not all young people have such possibility. In this case the Internet can be a spring of such information. I mean the Internet is not only for finding scientific information, but can be as a spring of just communication. I think it will be helpful for your people too."

MILESTONE 4: *Progress with the Fund-raising Effort*

Building community support and raising the funds for the Cyber Café gift were the primary objectives of the Gift Committee in 2002 and 2003. After trying to meet the goal of raising $660,000 with all volunteers, BDSC hired Barbara Perin as the Development Director for one year in October 2002. Additional motivation came from Dushanbe, when on April 23, 2003, Dushanbe Mayor Ubaidulloev proclaimed that the plot of land that he had reserved for the Cyber Café in January 2001 would be kept vacant for only three more years, during which time the Cyber Café needed to be built.

With community presentations encouraging community support, the support of paid staff, and Mayor Ubaidulloev's decree, the Boulder community, local businesses, foundations, and other partnerships gained momentum. By the end of 2003, half of the funds were raised and the City of Boulder loan effort provided the vehicle to raise the remaining amount. BDSC also worked hard to migrate its business processes to a new level to support the increased number and amount of donations received and the anticipated expenses that will begin with the start of construction.

Also around this time, The Digital Development Partnership, the philanthropic division of Citrix Systems, Inc. generously offered to fund the technology portion of the Cyber Café. The mission of the Digital Development Partnership is to optimize the social and economic impact of information and communications technology initiatives for underserved communities by enabling global access to affordable application service provider (ASP) computing capabilities.

The final success of this critical "gear-shifting" period of time in late 2002 was BDSC's establishment of a first-ever formal Finance Committee, which completely overhauled the organization's accounting system, brought in professional-level software and accounting practices, and improved the flow of information and assets. BDSC volunteer Corine Hauser, CPA, donated many hours assisting in this process.

MILESTONE 5: *The Boulder City Council Lends a Helping Hand*

On December 16, 2003, the Boulder City Council passed a resolution pledging future revenues that the City receives from the Dushanbe Teahouse lease towards the BDSC Cyber Cafe reciprocal gift for Dushanbe. These revenues are currently being used by the City to pay off the loan used for construction of the Teahouse and to maintain a facility maintenance/replacement fund for the Teahouse. Once the original construction loan is paid off (estimated to occur around 2015), these proceeds can go toward the Cyber Cafe. The city resolution allowed BDSC to borrow up to $350,000 in private funds based on this future revenue stream.

Boulder, Colorado

(Photo courtesy of the Boulder Convention and Visitors Bureau)

Newly-elected 2004 BDSC Board of Direction Co-President Don Mock took the lead in proposing this innovative scheme to the City Council, which passed the measure with only one dissenting vote. "It would be rather unseemly for a wealthy city in the wealthiest country in the world to benefit economically from a gift from one of the 10 poorest nations and then not reciprocate," Boulder Mayor Will Toor said.[56]

MILESTONE 6: *Relationship-building*

The Gift Committee was reenergized by the City Council resolution. Now chaired by Vern Seieroe, its fund-raising campaign was bringing in increasing levels of donations from Boulder citizens, and new project partners and some committee members joined the effort. The committee identified two areas of focus to successfully complete the Cyber Café for Dushanbe project, in addition to ongoing fund-raising:

    1. Communication and relationship building with Dushanbe; and

    2. Phase II- Construction of the Cyber Café structure.

Five BDSC Gift Committee members and a partner traveled to Dushanbe February 5–14, 2004 to set in motion BDSC's intention to break ground for the Cyber Café gift later that year.

The team included Vern Seieroe (Gift Committee Chair), Mary Axe (of the BDSC Education Committee), David Barrett (Project Architect), Scott Raderstorf (Technology Committee Chair), Traver Gruen-Kennedy (Director of BDSC partner Digital Development Partnership-Citrix), and Bob Ferenc (on-site construction representative candidate).

Highlights of the trip included:

- Strengthening BDSC's relationship with Dushanbe Mayor Mahmadsaid Ubaidulloev, who attended a reception for the delegation and expressed interest in and support of our project. The group felt that the mayor would like BDSC to begin construction as soon as possible. He offered constructive suggestions regarding the orientation of the Cyber Café.

- Strengthening BDSC's relationship with US Ambassador to Tajikistan Richard Hoagland. Ambassador Hoagland is also supportive of our project; he hosted a reception in honor of the delegation.

- Mary Axe met with many librarians from various educational institutions in Dushanbe and was very well received. They were all excited and supportive of our plans and want to work with us. They offered to supply volunteers and also gave many suggestions as to the kinds of materials they would like to have. They especially would appreciate receiving materials that give information about their heritage and Tajik folk tales for the children.

- Bob Ferenc met with Catherine Wilkins, Project Director of the new US Embassy in Dushanbe, which is under construction. She advised him about construction procedures and possible obstacles. He also met with various suppliers and people knowledgeable about managing construction projects in Dushanbe.

MILESTONE 7: *Implementation (The Future)*

The implementation phase had several major sub-phases requiring specific expertise and leadership, as defined in the Business Plan and reflected in the Gift Committee budget. These included architectural design and development, construction, computer and Internet technology, education, restaurant/service, and Boulder artwork, landscape design, art acquisition, and an owners on-site construction liaison.

MILESTONE 8: *Operation (The Future)*

The Cyber Café offers an opportunity to provide ongoing resources to the people of Dushanbe that can contribute to Tajikistan's broad development goals. Depending on the interests of the Dushanbe city government and the continuing support of BDSC, a range of continuing services hosted by the Cyber Café is possible. These potential services, which could also promote the sustainability of the Cyber Café, include computer and information technology training; cultural, student, and educational ties and scholarships; health and wellness outreach; and business training. Moving in this direction will require agreement on two conditions: first, purpose; and, second, capacity.

The BDSC Education Committee is interested in working toward improving educational opportunities for citizens of Boulder's sister city in the context of BDSC's gift. It has discussed implementing a "BDSC Online Knowledge Center" that connects citizens of the two sister cities in educational projects and programs through applications and online tools such as Web pages, discussion boards, e-learning courses, and interactive video. This would enable people in the two sister cities to learn from, with, and about each other; collaborate on educational, professional, and special-interest projects; and build friendship.

Photo courtesy of Scott Raderstorf

The BDSC delegation that visited Dushanbe from February 5-14, 2004 to plan ground-breaking of the Cyber Café gift, from left to right: Vern Seieroe, Traver Gruen-Kennedy, Mary Axe, Bob Ferenc, Scott Raderstorf, and David Barrett.

PART 4

Resources

Glossary of Tajik Cultural Terms

Aini, Sadriddin	Famous 20th century Tajik writer and the father of Tajik literature
Allahu Akbar	(Arabic: "God is Great") carved into a west-facing beam near the front door of the *Choihona*. It is Arabic script, unlike the other ceiling beam Cyrillic inscriptions. Cyrillic is used for writing Tajiki.
Amu Darya	A river that flows through the territory of Uzbekistan, Turkmenistan, Tajikistan and Afghanistan
arabesque	A complex, ornate design of intertwined floral, foliate, and geometric figures
ash	A favorite Tajik rice dish with meat and carrots; can also be a soup (also *osh*)
atlas	All-silk satin weave Tajik cloth
balish	Pillow used for back support on low tables (*kat*s) used for seating in teahouses and other buildings
Basmachi movement	Central Asian national Islamic resistance movement which strongly opposed Soviet rule during and after the Bolshevik revolution
bozor	Market-place (Iranian Farsi: *bazar)*
bogh	Garden
Bukhara	A city in Uzbekistan, known as an important ancient center of Islamic culture
caravanserai	inn
chapan	Man's robe that is worn over the shoulders as an outer garment
chehel setoon	Famous Safavid palace in Isfahan, Iran. Also there was a *chehel sutun* in Bokhara
choi	Tea (Iranian Farsi, *chai*)
chorpoi	Low table for seating. Also called *kat* or *topchan*
choihona	Teahouse. Also: *choikhona, choykhane, chaikhane*
coffer	A recessed panel of a ceiling
CIS	Commonwealth of Independent States. Official designation of the former republics of the Soviet Union that remained loosely federated in economic and security matters after the Soviet Union disbanded as a unified state in 1991. Members in 1996 were Armenia, Azerbaijan, Belarus, Georgia, Kazakhstan, Kyrgyzstan, Moldova, Russia, Tajikistan, Turkmenistan, Ukraine, and Uzbekistan
CPSU	Communist Party of the Soviet Union
corpa	Quilt serving as padding on the *low table (chorpoi)*
Dari	A language of Afghanistan closely related to Tajiki and Iranian Farsi
Dushanbe	The capital of Tajikistan (Tajiki: "Monday")
eremurus	Foxtail lilies motif found in the *Choihona* ceramic tiles
faience	Earthenware decorated with colorful opaque glazes
Farsi	The Persian language
Faroghat Teahouse	Well-known teahouse in Dushanbe
Fergana valley	Fertile valley running through parts of Uzbekistan, Tajikistan, and Kyrgyzstan
ganch	Plaster (Iranian Farsi: *gatch*)
ganch kori	Traditional Iranian/Tajik carved plaster artistic medium
Ganjawi, Nizami	12th century poet who wrote romances in Farsi
Gharm	A town in central Tajikistan
ghaveh	(Farsi) coffee
ghaveh-khane	(Farsi) Coffee-house

ghirikh	Geometrical ornamental motif used in Islamic art
glasnost	(Russian) "public voicing." Applied in the Soviet Union beginning in 1987 to allow public discussion of issues and public access to information, initially intended as a means for the regime of Mikhail S. Gorbachev to publicize the need for political and economic reform
gol	Flower, rose, both in nature and as an artistic motif
golestan	Rose garden
Gorno-Badahshon	An autonomous province in Southern Tajikistan
Haft Peykar	See "the Seven Beauties"
hauz	Pool
Hudo hofiz	Good-bye (Persian Farsi: *khoda hafez*)
hukumat	District or city government
ibrik	Pitcher design, common in Islamic art. The *ibrik* is used for ritual purification. It can be seen in the Choihona's faience panels along the outside walls.
Ismaili	One of the more influential Shiite groups, emphasizing secrecy and certain gnostical ideas and split off from the main Shiite stream at the 7th generation of recognized successive leaders, in 765 A.D.
ikat	Central Asia's most prestigious and beautiful fabric, a dyed silk. Also called *abr* (Farsi: "cloud")
ivan	(Also: *iwan*) A rectangular chamber of a building open on one side and usually surmounted by a barrel vault
joma	A knee-long jacket worn by some Tajik men
kat	See *chorpoi*
khankah	Muslim monastery
Khayyam, Omar	Famous Persian poet (1048–1131) who lived in Nishapur, Persia (now Iran)
khomshurbo	Traditional Tajik meat and vegetable soup
Khujand	Formerly Leninobod, a city in northern Tajikistan
kishloq	Rural settlement, village (Uzbek: *kishlak*)
Kulob	City in southern Khatlon province of Tajikistan
kurta	Tajik women's garment made of soft, colorful, bright silk
Leninobod	The former name of Khujand
madrasseh	(Arabic) An Islamic religious school
mahalla	(Arabic) Neighborhood, district
mantu	Traditional Tajik food, pasta stuffed with meat and spices
masjid	(Arabic) Mosque
mei (mey)	(Farsi) Wine
mey-khaneh	(Farsi) Wine house, tavern
mihrab	Prayer niche, usually in a religious building, indicating the direction of Mecca
Milashevich, Milan	Sculptor of "The Seven Beauties" sculpture in the Boulder-Dushanbe Teahouse
Mohammad	The prophet and founder of Islam who was born and lived in Saudi Arabia from 572–632
mionband	Kerchief worn by some Tajik men around the waist
mullah	A Muslim scholar and teacher
navruz	Tajiki-Persian New Year (Iranian Farsi: *noruz*)
NIS	Newly Independent States
oblast	(Russian) Administrative division consisting of districts and headed by the chairperson (*hokim*) appointed by the President (Tajik: *viloyat*)
osh	See *ash*

pakhsa	Beaten clay used in early building
Pamir	A plateau in Asia where the Hindu Kush, Tien Shan and Himalayas Mountain Ranges converge
Pamiris	The Pamiris, also known as Badakhshanis, reside in the Gorno-Badakhshan province. They are Tajiks but differ from the rest of the Tajik population by the fact that they speak several distinct Iranian languages and have a distinct culture. The Pamiris number in the tens-of-thousands. (Source: *The Tajik Update,* www.angelfire.com/sd/tajikistanupdate/culture.html)
partridge	Bird motif found in the *Choihona's* ceramic faience panels
perestroika	(Russian) "Restructuring" Applied in the late 1980s to an official Soviet program of revitalization of the Communist Party of the Soviet Union (CPSU), the economy, and the society by adjusting economic, social, and political mechanisms in the central planning system. Identified with the tenure of Mikhail S. Gorbachev as leader of the Soviet Union.
Persian	A member of the Iranian subgroup in the Indo-European language family that is the official language (Farsi) of modern Iran. Tajiki, which is written in Cyrillic, is closely related to standard Iranian Farsi, which is written using the Arabic script.
piyola	A small bowl used for drinking tea in Tajikistan
plov	Traditional Tajik pilaf
pomegranate	Popular motif used in Islamic art
Qurghonteppa	A city in southern Khatlon province Of Tajikistan
Raees (Rais)	Chairman, boss, head of an administrative or social unit
Rahmat	Thank you
Rahmonov, Imomali	The current President of Tajikistan
Rastokhez	Tajik liberal-national movement
rayon	(Russian) (Tajik: *nohiya*) Administrative division headed by a chairperson (*hokim*)
Rohat Teahouse	One of the more popular teahouses in Dushanbe
Rudaki, Abu 'Abd Allah	One of the most important Iranian poets who served at the court of the Samanids of Bukhara from 874 to 999
Safavid	Persian dynasty that ruled from 1501–1736. The founder of the dynasty, Ismail Safavi, crowned himself shah of Azerbaijan in 1501. The Safavids moved their capital to Isfahan, which, under Shah Abbas the Great, they beautified the city extensively.
Samanids	A dynasty of Tajik origin that ruled Central Asia in the 9th and 10th centuries from their capital in Bukhara
Samarkand	(Also: Samarqand) A city in the Eastern part of Uzbekistan that used to be Tamerlane's capital in the 14th century. Many Tajiks live there.
Saodat Teahouse	Poplar Dushanbe *choihona*
samovar	(Russian) Water-boiling tea-maker, often made of brass
samovarkhona	The place where tea is made and from which it is brought to guests in a house or *choihona*
"The Seven Beauties"	Name of Milan Milashevich's sculpture in the Boulder-Dushanbe Teahouse (Tajiki: *Haft Paykar*)
shalvor	Long pants with decorative cuffs worn by some Tajik women
shams	(Farsi, "sun") Large circular motif in Tajik embroidery, etc.
Shi'a	The smaller of the two great divisions of Islam, supporting the claims of Ali to leadership of the Muslim community, in opposition to the Sunni view of succession to Muslim leadership
shirchoi	Tajik tea with butter and milk
shurbo	Popular Tajik soup
sihkabob	Grilled meat on skewers

Soghdia	An historical region of Central Asia currently comprised of Southern Uzbekistan and Tajikistan
somoni	Tajik National currency
-stan	"Place of." The suffix *-stan* is formed from the Farsi root "*sta-* "to stand and means "place where one stays," i.e., homeland or country. Names such as Afghanistan and Tajikistan are formed by adding this suffix to the usually pluralized names of the people living in that country (Source: www.yourdictionary.com)
Sufi	A general term for a Muslim mystic and/or ascetic. Sufism refers to the mystical path of Islam in general
sumalak	National Tajik dish, made of raw wheat; usually prepared for *Navruz*
Sunni	The larger of the two fundamental divisions of Islam, opposed to the *Shi'a* on the issue of succession to Muslim leadership. Most Tajik Muslims are *Sunni*
suzaneh	Embroidery, also called *suzani*
Tajik	The language of Tajikistan, a person from Tajikistan, or the ethnic adjective. Also: Tajiki
talar	Veranda or raised porch
Tojik	How Tajiks say "Tajik"
Tojiki	How Tajiks say "Tajiki"
Tojikiston	How Tajiks say "Tajikistan"
toqii	Skullcap worn by Tajik men; its paisley design, distinguishes the wearers by region. Also: *tubeteika*
Turkestan	The term for Central Asia under Tsarist rule
Teymour	Tamerlane
topchan	(Russian) Low tables used for seating in Tajikistan. Normally called *chorpoi or kat*
tree of life	Common motif used in Islamic art
tubeteika	Embroidered Tajik skull cap worn by men and women
Ubaidulloev, Mahmadsaid	Current mayor of Dushanbe
Uzbeks	A Turkish race who originally were nomads that migrated to Central Asia Today the Uzbeks number roughly 1 million in Tajikistan and make up the second largest ethnic group after the Tajiks

Resources for Further Learning and Useful Contacts

The Boulder-Dushanbe Teahouse

The Boulder-Dushanbe Teahouse
www.boulderteahouse.com. 1770 13th Street, Boulder, Colorado. Phone: 303-442-4993.

The Boulder Rose Society
www.boulderrose.org

Boulder Garden Club (303) 443-9253.

Audio-tape interview with Tajik wood-carver Mirpulat Mirakhmatov. February 10, 1998. Robertson, Janet; Robertson, David; Axe, Mary; Seieroe, Vern; Sophia, Stoller; and Stoller, Peter. Carnegie Branch Library for Local History, Boulder, Colorado. Translated by Elmira Moukailova. (transcript is available)

Audio-tape interview with Tajik artist Kodir Rakhimov. February 10, 1998. Robertson, Janet; Robertson, David; Axe, Mary; Seieroe, Vern; Sophia, Stoller; and Stoller, Peter. Carnegie Branch Library for Local History, Boulder, Colorado. Translated by Elmira Moukailova. (transcript is available)

Audio-tape interview with Tajik ceramicist Viktor Zabolotnikov. March 23, 1998. Robertson, Janet; Robertson, David; Axe, Mary; Seieroe, Vern; Sophia, Stoller; and Stoller, Peter. Carnegie Branch Library for Local History: Boulder, Colorado. Translated by Elmira Moukailova. (transcript is available)

"Rocky Mountain Chai" by Joann Temple Dennett in *Aramco World*. November/December, 1998. Aramco Services, Houston. pp. 27-31.

Sister Cities

Boulder-Dushanbe Sister Cities
www.boulder-dushanbe.org. Phone: 303-444-9004 to make a donation, get information, or become a member.

Sister Cities International www.sister-cities.org.

Boulder-Lhasa (Tibet) Sister City Project
www.boulder-tibet.org

Boulder-Jalapa (Nicaragua)
www.ci.boulder.co.us/cmo/sistercities/jala.htm

Boulder-Mante (Mexico) Sister Cities
www.ci.boulder.co.us/cmo/sistercities/mante.htm

Boulder-Yamagata (Japan) Sister Friendship Committee http://bcn.boulder.co.us/community/yamagata

Boulder-Yateras (Cuba) Sister Cities
www.uscsca.org/boulderyateras.htm

The City of Boulder

Boulder Chamber of Commerce
www.boulderchamber.com

Boulder Convention and Visitors Bureau
www.bouldercoloradousa.com

Boulder City Government www.ci.boulder.co.us

Boulder County Government
www.co.boulder.co.us

Today's Weather in Boulder
www.weather.com/weather/local/USCO0038

Colorado University www.colorado.edu

Boulder Demographics www.boulderchamber.com/life/demographics.asp

The Daily Camera (newspaper)
www.thedailycamera.com

Boulder Webcam
http://9news.com/9live/boulder.asp

Pearl Street Webcam www.bouldercams.com

The City of Dushanbe

Bashiri, Iraj, "Dushanbe" www.angelfire.com/rnb/bashiri/Dushanbe/Dushanbe.html.

Welcome to Dushanbe www.geocities.com/
dushanbe2004. Personal Web site

The American Embassy in Dushanbe
http://usembassy.state.gov/dushanbe

Tajikistan – General Information and Internet Portals

**Republic of Tajikistan State Information
Agency** http://tajikistan.tajnet.com/english/
state/president.htm.

Iraj Bashiri's Portal www.angelfire.com/rnb/
bashiri/index.html. Iraj Bashiri is a professor
of Central Asian Studies at the University of
Minnesota. He is one of the most knowledgeable and respected experts on Tajikistan, Iran,
and other countries of Central Asia.

Tajnet http://tajikistan.tajnet.com/english/index.
html. Information and links about Tajikistan.

Tajikistan Update www.angelfire.com/sd/
tajikistanupdate. Cultural news, discussion
and chat groups, and a message board. Useful
information about Tajikistan.

**Central Intelligence Agency World Factbook
on Tajikistan** www.cia.gov/cia/publications/
factbook/geos/ti.html.

Soros Foundation www.soros.org/tajkstan.html.
News, facts, history, links related to Tajikistan
for the Central Asian and Eastern European
philanthropic fund and research organization.

Harvard Forum for Central Asian Studies
www.fas.harvard.edu/~centasia. A very useful
Central Asian studies site with resources and
links for scholars of Central Asia.

Tajik/Persian Art and Architecture

The cambridge history of iran by J.A. Boyle,
(Ed.). Cambridge University Press, 1968.

*Fabled cities of central asia: Samarkand,
bukhara, khiva by* Jacqueline Dector, (Ed.).
Abbevile Press, 1989.

The timurid architecture of iran and turan by
Lisa Golombek and Donald Wilber. Princeton
University Press, 1988.

The mediation of ornament by Oleg Grabar.
Princeton University Press, 1989.

Islamic architecture by John D. Hoag. Rizzoli, 1987.

*Timur and the princely vision: Persian art and
culture in the fifteenth century* by T. W.
Lorenz, & Glenn D. Lowry. Smithsonian
Institution Press, 1989.

Iran 1 by Anthony Hutt and Leonard Harrow.
Scorpion Publications, 1977.

*Survey of persian art from prehistoric time to
the present* by Arthur Upham Pope and Phyllis
Ackerman. Oxford University Press, 1939.

Persian architecture by Arthur Upham Pope.
Thames and Hudson, 1965.

Masterpieces of persian art by Arthur Upham
Pope. Greenwood Press, 1970.

The art of central asia by Galina Pucachenkova and
Akbar Khakimov. Aurora Art Publishers, 1988.

Islamic art by David Talbot Rice. Thames and
Hudson, 1965.

The images of paradise in islamic art by Sheila
S. Blair and Jonathan M. Bloom, (Eds.). Hood
Museum of Art, 1991.

Isfahan, pearl of persia by Wilfrid Blunt. Stein
and Day, 1966.

Web Sites

Archnet http://archnet.org/lobby.tcl. A site for
architects, planners, urban designers, interior
designers, landscape architects, and scholars,
with a special focus on the Islamic world.

Encyclopedia Iranica www.iranica.com. An
excellent online resource self-described as "the
most extensive compendium ever conceived
on the past and present culture of the people
who speak an Iranian language."

"Arts and Crafts in Transoxania and Khurasan" (Hakimov, A. A.) in UNESCO's *The History of the Civilization of Central Asia:* www.unesco.org/culture/asia/html_eng/chapitre4216/chapitre1.htm.

Iransaga www.art-arena.com. Provides a valuable insight into Persian history, art, and culture.

Islamic Arts and Architecture http://islamicart.com/index.html. Islamic Arts and Architecture (IAAO) is a non-profit organization dedicated to providing information on Islamic arts and architecture.

State Hermitage Museum (St. Petersburg, Russia) www.hermitagemuseum.org

Welcome to Isfahan http://isfahan.apu.ac.uk/isfahan.html. Virtual tour of Isfahan, Iran, a World Heritage City, with explanatory text.

Persian, Tajik and Islamic Gardens

Gardens of paradise: The history and design of great islamic gardens by John Brookes. Weidenfeld and Nicolson, 1987.

Persian Gardens and Garden Pavilions by Donald N.Wilbur. Tuttle, 1962.

"The Timurid Court: Life and Gardens and Tents" by Donald M., Wilber in *Journal of Persian Studies*, Vol. XVII, London (The British Institute of Persian Studies, 1979).

Tajik and Persian Poetry, Literature, and Music

Nizami: haft paykar, a medieval persian romance translated by J. S. Meisami. Oxford University Press, 1995.

"A Brief Note on Sadriddin Aini's Life" by Iraj Bashiri. www.angelfire.com/rnb/bashiri/AiniChron/Ainichrn.html

"The Rubaiyat of Omar Khayyam: A Complete Online Resource." www.therubaiyat.com

"Samuel Taylor Coleridge: Kubla Khan or, a Vision In a Dream: A Fragment." www.wsu.edu:8080/~wldciv/world_civ_reader/world_civ_reader_2/coleridge.html#1

"A Brief Note on the Life of Abu Abd Allah Rudaki" by Iraj Bashiri. www.angelfire.com/rnb/bashiri/Poets/Rudaki.html

Silk Road Project www.silkroadproject.org. Yo-Yo Ma's Silk Road Project site.

The Aga Khan Music Initiative in Central Asia www.akdn.org/Music/Musicin.htm

Tajik Music www.geocities.com/shaitov/tajikmusic.htm. "Music from Sunny Tajikistan." Includes many downloads and information about Tajik singers and song-writers.

Hundred thousand fools of god: The musical travels in central asia (and queens, new york) by Theodore Levin. Bloomington Indiana University Press, 1999.

UNESCO Collection of Traditional Music of the World: Tajikistan www.unesco.orgculture/cdmusic/html_eng/tajik.shtml

Prominent tajik figures of the twentieth century by Iraj Bashiri. International Borbad Foundation, 2002. Excellent resource.

Tajik and Persian Tea and Food
Publications

The book of tea by Kakuzo Okakura. Dover, 1964. Every tea-lover must read this little book.

New food of life: Ancient persian and modern iranian cooking and ceremonies by Najimieh Batmanglij. Mage Publishers, 1997. Great cookbook with lots of food-related cultural information.

The legendary cuisine of persia by Margaret Shaida. Lieuse Publications, 1992. Like *New Food for Life* (above), this is a treasure of food and beverage-related facts and recipes. It, too, contains mouth-watering photos of traditional Persian dishes.

New tea lover's treasury by James Norwood Pratt. PTA: 1999.

The world of caffeine: The science and culture of the world's most popular drug by Bennett Alan Weinberg, and Bonnie K. Bealer. Routledge, 2001.

The afternoon tea book by Michael Smith. MacMillan, 1989.

Consumption and the making of respectability, 1600–1800 by Woodruff D. Smith. Routledge, 2003.

Taking tea by Andrea Israel. Grover Press, 1989.

Web Sites

Bashiri, Iraj, "Tea for Two." www.angelfire. com/rnb/bashiri/Teahouse/Tea42.html. An excellent article about Tajik teahouses and Tajik tea customs.

Tea - A Magazine. www.connix.com/~teamag

James Norwood Pratt Society www.jnptea.com. One of many excellent "tea portals" on the web by the author of a book on tea.

Celestial Seasonings www.celestialseasonings. com. Boulder-based tea purveyor company Web site with lots of information about tea.

Herb Research Foundation www.herbs.org. A wealth of information about the health benefits and safety of medicinal plants, including tea by this Boulder non-profit located at 1007 Pearl Street, Suite 200, Boulder, CO 80302; Phone (303) 449-2265.

Tea Market Report www.vanrees.com/ market_report.htm

Tea & Coffee Trade Journal www.teaand coffee.net

Health News about Tea www.celestialseasonings. com/research/newsaboutherbstea.php

Tajik History

The samanids and the revival of the civilization of the iranian peoples. (Bashiri, Iraj): Samanid World Symposium, 1998.

"Tajikistan: An Overview" (Bashiri, Iraj): www.angelfire.com/rnb/bashiri/Tajikistan/Taj. html. A comprehensive Web site about Central Asia and Iran.

Civil society in central asia. (Ruffin, M. Holt, and Waugh, Daniel (Editors). The University of Washington Press, 1998. An excellent resource about modernization in Tajikistan and Central Asia.

"Tajikistan in the 20th Century" www.rferl.org/ bd/ta/special/20century/index.html. Audio series on Contemporary History of Tajikistan, presented by Salimjon Aioubov, on the Radio Free Europe/Radio Liberty Web site.

"Tajikistan Update" www.angelfire.com/sd/ tajikistanupdate. A clearinghouse of many things Tajik.

Tajik and Persian Area Studies

Isfahan, pearl of persia by Wilfrid Blunt. Stein and Day, 1966.

Iranian culture: A persianist view by John Hillmann. University Press of America, 1990.

The history of modern iran: An Interpretation by Joseph M. Upton. Harvard University Press, 1965.

The bazaar by Walet M. Weiss and Kurt-Michael Wetermann. Thames and Hudson, 1994. Superb reading and photos.

Jewish history of tajikistan www.heritagefilms.com/TAJIKISTAN.html

An abridged history of central asia by William Brinton. www.asian-history.com/the_frame.html

Shorter encyclopaedia of islam by H. A. R Gibb and J. H. Kramers (Leiden (E. J. Brill, 1974).

Tajik International Olympic Committee.
www.olympic.org/uk/organisation/noc/
noc_uk.asp?noc_initials=TJK

An account of a 1992 mountaineering expedition to the Pamirs http://chezphil.org/
gallery/1992_Pamirs/index.html

Radio Liberty: Listen to live RFE/RL Radio broadcasts in Tajiki http://www.rferl.org/listen

UNESCO Photos www.unesco.org/webworld/
asicent/taj.htm. A wonderful collection of photos of Tajikistan.

Tajik Clothes www.iles.umn.edu/faculty/
bashiri/Costume.html

Tajik Jewelry www.iles.umn.edu/faculty/
bashiri/Jewelry.html

Tajnet http://tajikistan.tajnet.com/
english/aboutland/gallery.htm. Photo site.

Tajik and Central Asian Current Events, Politics, and News

US Department of State Country Report on Human Rights Practices in Tajikistan
www.state.gov/g/drl/rls/hrrpt/2002/18395.htm

Asia-Plus www.internews.ru/ASIA-PLUS. An independent news service in Tajikistan.

Eurasianet www.eurasianet.org/resource/
tajikistan/index.shtml. News, discussion groups, articles.

IRIN News www.irinnews.org. United Nations site "focuses on strengthening universal access to timely, strategic and non-partisan information so as to enhance the capacity of the humanitarian community to understand, respond to and avert emergencies."

The Times of Central Asia www.times.kg.
Online newspaper from Kazakhstan.

Radio Free Europe/Radio Liberty www.rferl.org/
reports/centralasia/archive2004.asp and
www.rferl.org/newsline/2-tca.asp. Large site with lots of news, special reports, and RealAudio files.

Tajnet tajikistan.tajnet.com/english/news.htm

The Research Institute for Inner Asian Studies (RIFIAS) www.indiana.edu/~rifias.
Electronic library catalogs of manuscripts containing historical, biographical, and geographical information on Islamic and Central Asia.

Tajik Non-Government Organizations (NGOs) and Humanitarian Organizations

CANGO Central Asian NGO Database for Tajikistan. www.cango.net/db

Counterpart www.counterpart.org/.
Counterpart's Community and Humanitarian Assistance Program (CHAP) builds strong civil societies in emerging nations by helping to meet humanitarian and development needs of the most vulnerable members of society.

IREX www.irex.org/internet.The International Research & Exchanges Board specializes in education, independent media, Internet development, and civil society programs in Central Asia and many other regions.

The Aga Khan Foundation www.akdn.org/
agency/akf.html. A non-denominational development agency established in 1967 whose mission is "to develop and promote creative solutions to problems that impede social development, primarily in Asia and East Africa."

Mercy Corps http://www.mercycorps.org.
Mercy Corps is a not-for-profit organization that exists to alleviate suffering, poverty, and oppression by helping people build secure, productive, and just communities.

Open Society Institute (Soros Foundation)
http://www.soros.org. Implements a range of initiatives that aim to promote open societies "by shaping government policy and supporting education, media, public health, and human and women's rights, as well as social, legal, and economic reform.".

Tajiki Language

Tajik-english/english-tajik dictionary & phrasebook by Joseph Conroy. Hippocrene Books, 1998.

Persian vocabulary by A. K. S. Lambton. Cambridge University Press, 1966.

Persian grammar by A. K. S. Lambton. Cambridge University Press, 1966.

Accounts of Western Travelers to Central Asia

The travels of marco polo by Marco Polo. (Translated by W. Marsden). Dell, 1961. [Travel in 1271].

Travels in asia and africa: 1325–1354 by Ibn Battuta. New Delhi, 1929. [Travel in the 14th century].

A relation of some yeares travaile by Sir Thomas Herbert. Related in "The First English Guide Book to Persia," in *Journal of Persian Studies*, Vol. XV. The British Institute of Persian Studies, 1977. [Travel in 1634].

A journey to persia by Sir Jean Chardin. (Translated by Ronald W. Ferrier). I. B. Tauris, 1996. [Travel in 1723].

The adventures of hajji baba of ispahan by James Morrier. Oxford University Press, 1963. [Travel in 1824].

Captain sir richard burton by Edward Rice. Scribner's, 1990. [Travel in mid 19th century].

A year amongst the persians by Edward Granville Browne. Hippocrene Books, Inc., 1984. [Travel in 1887].

Journeys in persia and kurdistan by Isabella Bird Bishop. Random House, 1988. [Travel in 1891].

The road to oxiana by Robert Byron. Oxford University Press, 1982. [Travel in 1933].

Foreign devils on the silk road by Peter Hopkirk. University of Massachusetts, 1980. [20th century travel].

Web Sites Facilitating Education and Communication between Americans and Tajiks

Boulder-Dushanbe Sister Cities Discussion Board boulder-dushanbe.org/cgi-local/yabb/YaBB.pl.

IREX (the International Research & Exchanges Board) www.irex.org. US non-profit organization specializing in education, independent media, Internet development, and civil society programs in the United States, Europe, Eurasia, the Middle East and North Africa, and Asia.

Internet Access Training Project (IATP) http://iatp.irex-tj.org/EN/index.php. IATP is a program of the Bureau of Educational and Cultural Affairs (ECA) of the US Department of State. IATP provides free Internet access and training in 11 countries throughout Central Asia, the Caucasus, and Western Eurasia.

School Connectivity Project for Central Asia www.connect-tajikistan.org. Establishing 20 Internet learning centers in secondary schools across Tajikistan.

Linux Tajik Translation Project http://68.54.23.240/translation.shtml. Roger Kovacs' project to create Tajik language software (Khujand Computer Technologies). With a link to an associated Tajik NGO Youth Opportunities.

American Councils for International Education/ACCELS Tajikistan Office and Educational Advising Center www.actr.org/eic/dushanbe

Source Notes

1 (Gluck, Siver, and Gluck 1996)
2 (Pucachenkova & Khakimov 1988, 11)
3 (Woodbridge 1991, 8)
4 (Pucachenkova & Khakimov 1988, plate 5)
5 (Pucachenkova & Khakimov 1988)
6 (Kodir Rakhimov. Interview with Janet Robertson, David Robertson, Mary Axe, Vern Seieroe, Sophia Stoller, and Peter Stoller, February 10, 1998. Tape 1, Side A, Section 10. Carnegie Branch Library for Local History: Boulder Colorado. Translated by Elmira Moukailova)
7 (Kodir Rakhimov. Interview with Janet Robertson, David Robertson, Mary Axe, Vern Seieroe, Sophia Stoller, and Peter Stoller, February 10, 1998. Tape 1, Side A, Section 10. Carnegie Branch Library for Local History: Boulder, Colorado. Translated by Elmira Moukailova)
8 (Kodir Rakhimov. Interview with Janet Robertson, David Robertson, Mary Axe, Vern Seieroe, Sophia Stoller, and Peter Stoller, February 10, 1998. Tape 1, Side A, Section 70. Carnegie Branch Library for Local History, Boulder, Colorado. Translated by Elmira Moukailova)
9 (Sarhangi 199, 87)
10 (Weiss & Wetermann 1994, 115)
11 (Pucachenkova & Khakimov 1988, 160)
12 (Mirpulat Mirakhmatov. Interview with Janet Robertson, David Robertson, Mary Axe, Vern Seieroe, Sophia Stoller, and Peter Stoller, February 10, 1998. Tape 1, Side B, Section 128. Carnegie Branch Library for Local History, Boulder, Colorado. Translated by Elmira Moukailova)
13 (Kodir Rakhimov. Interview with Janet Robertson, David Robertson, Mary Axe, Vern Seieroe, Sophia Stoller, and Peter Stoller, February 10, 1998. Tape 1, Side A, Section 395. Carnegie Branch Library for Local History, Boulder, Colorado. Translated by Elmira Moukailova)
14 (Pope 1965, 147)
15 (Gluck, Siver, and Gluck 1996, 4)
16 (Dector 1989, 77)
17 (Viktor Zabolotnikov. Interview with Janet Robertson, David Robertson, Mary Axe, Vern Seieroe, Sophia Stoller, and Peter Stoller, March 23, 1998. Tape 1, Side B, Section 442. Carnegie Branch Library for Local History: Boulder, Colorado. Translated by Elmira Moukailova)
18 (Viktor Zabolotnikov. Interview with Janet Robertson, David Robertson, Mary Axe, Vern Seieroe, Sophia Stoller, and Peter Stoller, March 23, 1998. Tape 1, Side B, Section 40. Carnegie Branch Library for Local History: Boulder, Colorado. Translated by Elmira Moukailova)
19 (Viktor Zabolotnikov. Interview with Janet Robertson, David Robertson, Mary Axe, Vern Seieroe, Sophia Stoller, and Peter Stoller, March 23, 1998. Tape 1, Side A, Section 554. Carnegie Branch Library for Local History, Boulder, Colorado. Translated by Elmira Moukailova)
20 (Pope 1965, 236)
21 (Dennett 1998, 27-31)
22 (ibid. 27-31)
23 (Okakura 1964, 18)
24 (Chardin 1988)
25 (Gibb &Gibb 1986, 46)
26 (ibid, 30-31)
27 (E-mail to author from Firuz Khlaimdjonov, October 24, 2003)
28 (E-mail to author from Dilorom Asimova, November 27, 1999)
29 (http://www.whitehorsetavern.com)
30 (Gibb &Gibb 1986)
31 (Bashiri 2000. "Two for Tea". Retrieved February 28, 2004, from http://www.angelfire.com/rnb/bashiri/Teahouse/Tea42.)
32 (Pope 1970)
33 ("Garden," Iranica Web site: http://www.iranica.com/articles/v10f3/v10f390a.html)
34 (Dector. 1989, 99)
35 (Smith 2003, 151)
36 (Weinberg & Bealer 2001, 39)
37 (http://www.liptont.com/about_tea/histor_tea/index.asp)
38 (http://www.liptont.com/about_tea/histor_tea/index.asp)
39 (Adapted from: http://www.cjn.or.jp/karakuri/serve-tea-1.html)
40 (http://www.easterntea.com/tea/asiantea.htm# compressed)
41 (http://www.liptont.com/about_tea/histor_tea/index.asp)
42 (Bashiri, Iraj (2000). "Two for Tea," 2)
43 ("Two Cancer Studies: Tomatoes, Green Tea, and Cancer." P&S Journal: Fall 1997, Vol. 17, No. 3)
44 Heartcenteronline, November 13, 2000. http://www.heartcenteronline.com/myheartdr/home/research-detail.cfm?reutersID=404).
45 (Epidemiology 2001 Nov; 12(6):695-700)
46 (Hey, Mary. Ten Years and a Teahouse," Pamphlet distributed at the BDSC1983-1993)
47 (ibid)
48 (ibid)
49 (Allen, Joe, in an e-mail to the author, March 15, 2004)
50 (Bashiri 2002, 127)
51 (Protocol by and between the City of Boulder Colorado and Dushanbe, Tadzhikistan, September 11, 1990)
52 (See http://www.berlin-hidden-places.de/yuba_web3/sachindex_en/cafe-mit_tadshik_en.htm)
53 ("Task force calls for more study abroad" CNN, Nov.19, 2003) Retrieved March 2, 2004, from http://www.cnn.com/2003/EDUCATION/11/19/study.abroad.ap/index.html)
54 (ibid.)
55 (http://www.silkroadproject.org)
57 (Avery, Greg, "Council Pledges Rent for Gift, Daily Camera, December 17, 2003)

Bibliography

Aioubov, Salimjon. Tajikistan in the 20th century (Audio series). http://www.rferl.org/bd/ta/special/20century/index.html.

Arberry, A.J. (1953). *The legacy of persia*. Oxford: Clarendon Press.

Bashiri, Iraj (1997). Dushanbe. Retrieved February 21, 2004, from http://www.angelfire.com/rnb/bashiri/Dushanbe/Dushanbe.html

Bashiri, Iraj (1998). *The Samanids and the revival of the civilization of Iranian peoples*. Dushanbe: World Symposium.

Bashiri, Iraj (1998). Tajik costumes. Retrieved February 8, 2004, from http://www.iles.umn.edu/faculty/bashiri/Costume.html

Bashiri, Iraj (1999). "Tajikistan: An Overview". Retrieved February 28, 2004, from www.angelfire.com/rnb/bashiri/Tajikistan/Taj.html

Bashiri, Iraj (2000). A tale of two cities. Retrieved February 28, 2004, from http://www.angelfire.com/rnb/bashiri/Teahouse/2cities.html.

Bashiri, Iraj (2000). Two for tea. Retrieved February 28, 2004, from http://www.angelfire.com/rnb/bashiri/Teahouse/Tea42.

Bashiri, Iraj (2000). The teahouse at a glance. Retrieved February 28, 2004, from http://www.angelfire.com/rnb/bashiri/Teahouse/Figures.html.

Bashiri, Iraj (2002). *Prominent tajik figures of the twentieth century*. Dushanbe: International Borbad Foundation. (Also http://www.angelfire.com/rnb/bashiri/TajikFigures/TajikFigures.pdf).

Blair, Sheila S. & Bloom, Jonathan M. (Eds.) (1991). *The images of paradise in islamic art*. Hanover, NH: Hood Museum of Art.

Blunt, Wilfrid (1966). *Isfahan, pearl of persia*. New York: Stein and Day.

Boyle, J.A., (Editor). (1968). *The Cambridge History of Iran*. Cambridge: Cambridge University Press.

Brookes, John (1987). *Gardens of paradise: The history and design of great islamic gardens*. London: Weidenfeld and Nicolson.

CIA world factbook on tajikistan. http://www.cia.gov/cia/publications/factbook/geos/ti.html.

Chardin, Sir John. (1988). *Travels in persia*, 1673–1677. Reprint of 1927 edition. Mineola, New York: Dover Publications.

Conroy, Joseph. (1998). *Tajik-english/English tajik dictionary & phrasebook*. New York: Hippocrene Books.

Dector, Jacqueline (Editor) (1989). *Fabled cities of central asia: Samarkand, bukhara, khiva*. New York: Abbevile Press.

Dennett, Joann Temple. (1998). "Rocky Mountain Chai" in *Aramco World*. November/December, 1998. Aramco Services, Houston. pp.27–31.

Duffy, Stephen J., *et. al.* (2001, July 10). Short- and long-term black tea consumption reverses endothelial dysfunction in patients with coronary artery disease in *Circulation: The Journal of the American Heart Association*. Retrieved March 16, 2004, from http://circ.ahajournals.org/content/vol104/issue2

Ford, P. R. J. (1989) *The oriental carpet: a history and guide to traditional motifs, patterns, and symbols*. New York: Portland House.

"Garden," retrieved December 11, 2003 from the Iranica Web site: http://www.iranica.com/articles/v10f3/v10f390a.html

Gibb, H. A. R. & Kramers, J. H. (1974). *Shorter Encyclopaedia of Islam*. Leiden: E. J. Brill.

Gibb, A. R. and Gibb, H. A. R. (1986). *Ibn Battuta: Travels in Asia and Africa 1325-1354*. Columbia. MO: South Asia Books.

Gluck, J. Siver, Noel, and Gluck, S. M. (Editors) (1996). *Surveyors of persian art from prehistoric time to the present*. Mazda.

Golombek, Lisa and Wilber, Donald (1988). *The timurid architecture of iran and turan*. Princeton University Press

Grabar, Oleg. (1989). *The mediation of ornament*. Princeton University Press.

Herbert, Sir Thomas. *A relation of some yeares travaile*. Related in The First English Guide Book to Persia in *Journal of Persian Studies*, Vol. XV. London: The British Institute of Persian Studies, 1977.

Hillmann, John (1990). *Iranian culture: A persianist view*. NewYork: University Press of America.

Hooker, Richard. What is kabuki? Washington State University. Retrieved February 28, 2004, from http://www.wsu.edu:8080/~dee/KABUKI/WHATIS.HTM

Khayyam, Omar (1983). *The rubaiyyat of omar khayyam*. New York: St. Martin's Press.

Knopf, Jim (2003). *The xeriscape flower gardener: A waterwise guide for the rocky mountain region*. Boulder, CO: Johnson Books.

Lorenz, T. W. & Lowry, G. D. (1989). *Timur and the princely vision; Persian art and culture in the fifteenth century*. Washington, D.C.: Smithsonian Institution Press.

Mann, Poonam (2001, February) Fighting Terrorism: India and Central Asia. *Strategic Analysis*, Volume XXVI, Number 11. Retrieved March 23, 2004 from http://www.ciaonet.org/olj/ad/ad_v7_3/kig01.html.

Matheson, S. A. (1972). *Persia: An archeological guide*. London: Faber and Faber.

Morris, James, Wood, Roger, &Wright, Denis. (1969). *Iran*. Tehran: I. A. D. A. Limited.

Okakura, Kakuzo (1964). *The book of tea*. New York: Dover.

Pope, Arthur Upham (1934). The Historic Significance of Stucco Decoration in Persian Architecture. In *The Art Bulletin*, Vol. XVI. New York: American Institute for Persian Art and Archeology.

Pope, Arthur Upham (1965). *Persian architecture*. London: Thames and Hudson.

Pope, Arthur Upham (1970). *Masterpieces of persian art*. Westport, CT: Greenwood Press.

Pucachenkova, Galina, & Khakimov, Akbar (1988). *The art of central asia*. Leningrad: Aurora Art Publishers.

Rahmatullaeva, Sulhiniso (n.d.). The Peculiarities of Samanid decorative architecture. Edited and translated by Iraj Bahiri. Retrieved January 6, 2004, from http://ilasll.unm.edu/bashiri/Suhl%20flder/suhl.html.

Rice, David Talbot. (1965) *Islamic art*. London: Thames and Hudson.

Robertson, Janet; Robertson, David; Axe, Mary; Seieroe, Vern; Sophia, Stoller, and Stoller, Peter. Audio-taped interview with Mirpulat Mirakhmatov. February 10, 1998. Carnegie Branch Library for Local History, Boulder, Colorado. Translated by Elmira Moukailova.

Robertson, Janet; Robertson, David; Axe, Mary; Seieroe, Vern; Sophia, Stoller; and Stoller, Peter. Audio-taped interview with Kodir Rakhimov. February 10, 1998. Carnegie Branch Library for Local History, Boulder, Colorado. Translated by Elmira Moukailova,

Robertson, Janet; Robertson, David; Axe, Mary; Seieroe, Vern; Sophia, Stoller; and Stoller, Peter. Audio-taped interview with Viktor Zabolotnikov, March 23, 1998. Carnegie Branch Library for Local History: Boulder, Colorado. Translated by Elmira Moukailova.

Ruffin, M. Holt, & Waugh, Daniel (editors) (1998). *Civil society in central asia*. London: The University of Washington Press.

Sarhangi, R. (1999) "The Sky Within: Mathematical Aesthetics of Persian Dome Interiors" in *Nexus, The International Journal of Architecture and Mathematics*.

Shah, Idries (1971). *The Sufis*. New York: Anchor.

Smith, Michael (1989). *The afternoon tea book*. New York: MacMillan.

Smith, Woodruff D. (2003) *Consumption and the making of respectability*, 1600–1800. New York: Routledge.

Sneider, Vern (1951). *The teahouse of the august moon*. New York: Putnam's.

Task force calls for more study abroad. *CNN*, Nov.19, 2003. Retrieved March 2, 2004, from http://www.cnn.com/2003/EDUCATION/11/19/study.abroad.ap/index.html)

Tea May Benefit Blood Vessels. (2000, November 13). *Heartcenteronline*. Retrieved March 16, 2004, from http://www.heartcenteronline.com/myheartdr/home/research-detail.cfm?reutersID=404.

Two cancer studies: tomatoes, green tea, and cancer. (Fall, 1997). *P&S Journal*, Vol. 17, No.3. Retrieved March 16, 2004, from http://cpmcnet.columbia.edu/news/journal/journal-o/archives/jour_v17n03_0009.html.

Weinberg, Bennett Alan & Bealer, Bonnie K. (2001). *The world of caffeine: The science and culture of the world's most popular drug*. New York: Routledge.

Weiss, Walet M. & Wetermann, Kurt-Michael (1994). *The bazaar*. London (Thames and Hudson).

Wilbur, Donald (1962). *Persian gardens and garden pavilions*. Rutland, Vermont: Tuttle.

Wilber, Donald (1979). The Timurid Court: Life and Gardens and Tents in *Journal of Persian Studies*, Vol. XVII. London: The British Institute of Persian Studies.

Woodbridge, Sally B. (1991). *Details: The architect's art*. San Francisco: Chronicle Books.

Index